THE COMPLETE
SHIBA INU

Maureen Atkinson

Howell Book House

HOWELL
BOOK
HOUSE

HOWELL BOOK HOUSE
A Simon & Schuster / Macmillan Company
1633 Broadway
New York, NY 10019

MACMILLAN is a registered trademark of Macmillan, Inc.

Library of Congress Cataloging-in-Publication Data
available on request

ISBN 0–87605–177–8

Manufactured in Singapore

10 9 8 7 6 5 4 3 2 1

CONTENTS

PREFACE

The Japanese Shiba Inu is the most wonderful and captivating breed. These dogs are truly unique in many ways, but only by owning one can you fully appreciate this. While being all dog, they have an uncanny understanding of the human and, without being gushy, they convey that understanding in many, many ways.

Though it is still relatively new to us here in England, we thirst for knowledge and information about the breed. Only by communicating with other Shiba lovers do we gradually put a picture together – through our own experience, and the experience of others, this can happen. The origins of the breed are steeped in Japan's history. The language barrier makes it difficult to gain information easily. If only those with Japanese connections were more forthcoming with their knowledge, then we could all benefit. For we still have much to learn and will go on learning for many years to come.

Much of the background to the Shiba Inu has come from America to us – as did our first Shiba Inu Imports, and for this we must be eternally grateful. Terry Arndt, Gretchen Haskett and Susan Houser all deserve a special mention, for they have been unstinting in their work to bring information to the masses worldwide, through *The Shiba Journal*.

I would like to thank Gerald and Kath Mitchell for introducing me to the Shiba and for their help and support in the beginning. Also my thanks to Les and Ranee Crawley who helped with the setting up of The Japanese Shiba Inu Club in 1987; those were memorable days.

Many people have contributed information and photographs for this book, both here and abroad, and I would like to thank them for their contributions. My thanks to Wendy Harris of the Eastbourne and District Agility Club for setting up a course and allowing photographs to be taken at her home.

In particular, I would like to say a big 'Thank You' to Lyn Lane, who has supported me and the Shiba for many years. Her continued help and commitment to me and to the Shiba has

The Shiba Inu: A most wonderful and captivating breed.

been unwavering. Without her help and researching, the task of compiling this book would have been monumental.

Lastly, I would like to say that I have done my best to put all of my own experience of the breed into this book. There may be things you do not agree with, or have experienced to the contrary. Much time and research has gone into producing this account of the Shiba. Any errors or omissions I gladly take on board and apologise for. Human error is a failing we all have. I hope that when you have read the book you will find something that will be of use to you, for we are all students and are forever learning.

Maureen Atkinson.

1 ORIGINS OF THE JAPANESE SHIBA INU

Some early writings mention the wolves of Japan. There were two kinds, though now there are none. One of the subspecies of Grey Wolf was the Yeso Wolf which, although it is now extinct in Japan, is said to survive still in Russia. The other subspecies was a 'miniature' Japanese Wolf; the Japanese called it the Shamanu. Although the Shamanu is now classified as a Grey Wolf, a 19th century natural historian, called Temminck, gave this 'miniature' Grey Wolf the name *Canis Hodophilax* . He and some other early observers felt that it differed so much from the other Grey Wolf that it should have a specific classification of its own. The *Canis*

Hodophilax had very distinct characteristics which suggested that it had been isolated in Japan for a long time.

The Shamanu was the world's smallest wolf. It measured 84cm (2ft 9in) in length, and it had a dog-like tail that measured 12in. It had a short, dense-haired coat, ash-grey in colour, with tinges of white, russet and brown. Some yellowish, brown and whitish-grey skins were also recorded. More unusual, however, was the Shamanu's height; he measured 39cm. (14in) at the shoulder. His legs were extraordinarily short for any real wolf. Wolves are tall. Thus, characteristically, he was more closely related to the wild dog than to the Grey

The Miniature Japanese Wolf – the Shamanu.

Illustration: Phillipa Coxall. First reproduced in All About Dogs.

Wolf. Though small in stature, the Shamanu was greatly feared by the Ainus, the aboriginal Japanese people. They called him the 'Howling God' because he often howled for hours from the hilltops and mountains. Homes in the North of Japan, as well as having a notice giving the street number and family details, displayed a charm to keep the wolves away from their doors. The Japanese fear of the 'miniature' wolf far outweighed the actual threat this animal presented. Sadly for the Shamanu, this obsessional fear would be detrimental to their survival and led to their downfall.

Shamanus were hunted and trapped persistently for their skins; they were also offered for sale to gluttonous Europeans. The main stronghold of the Shamanu was in Honshu, but they were also numerous in Hokkaido and the Kuriles – regions which operated a bounty for the Shamanu. In Hokkaido, in the years between 1878-1882, the local government bounty was seven yen; after 1888 it was ten yen. In 1905 a Shamanu was killed near Washikaguchi in Honshu and its skin was presented to a European traveller, Malcolm P. Anderson. Eventually it ended up in the Natural History Museum in London, donated by the Duke of Bedford. That was the last the world saw of the Japanese wolf called the Howling God.

THE PURE JAPANESE DOG
What kind of dog is the pure Japanese breed of dog, or *Canis Familiaris*? From archaeological and zoological studies made, it would appear that the ancient mammals that lived in Japan were of a large size, namely deer, bear, boar and the wild dog. This was also the case in Europe and America. The wild dogs became man's associate in many ways and proved to be of great use to him. Mammals' bones that have been excavated from old tombs and shell mounds in various parts of Japan were said to be the remains of the food of the then inhabitants; the bones were mainly that of the deer, bear and boar. But archaeologists also found bones of the dog suggesting that they, too, were used for food. The bones had been cut in regular joints, as is done in food preparation. However, excavated earthenware used by the ancient people of Japan has carvings depicting large animals being chased by dogs – thus confirming man's use of the dog to hunt other animals.

Skeletal remains of a small dog with a curled tail were discovered by archaeologists in the ruins of the Jomon Period (8,000 – 200 BC). Many Japanese scholars have expressed the opinion that the pure-bred specimen of the *Canis Familiaris Japonicus* is the breed now known as the Shiba Inu. Its isolation in remote areas of Japan probably resulted in its preservation in its original form. Primitive drawings and carvings which have been found show that a Shiba-like dog existed in the third century BC.

The *Canis Familiaris Japonicus* is thought to be one of the Northern strains traced through zoological facts linking prehistoric Japan with Asia – of the strains found, the smaller is felt to be the true prototype Shiba Inu, for though smaller, it is strong and sturdily built. The larger strain is thought to be that of the Akita Inu.

THE EFFECTS OF TRADE

During the Middle Ages, Japan had contact with countries such as Korea, China and Holland. In those days these mutual dealings were of little significance and would have had little or no influence on the native dog of Japan. But when, in the 19th century, the Great Emperor Meiji opened Japan's doors to commerce with western nations, many aspects of Japanese life changed and the cross-breeding of its dogs took place. With the extreme westernising of the nation every aspect of social, cultural and everyday life underwent great changes. Even the pure Japanese breed of dog gradually began to disappear.

Many foreign dogs came into the country, of many different breeds. The Japanese people admired these foreign dogs and began to interbreed them with their own native dogs. They gave no thought to the fact that they were losing their own pure breed. Only the dogs living in the mountainous regions escaped this crossbreeding. Then as Japanese society became more modernised and organised, the people began to look to their own culture once more. Preservation and protection became an important issue to them. Their native dog was recognised as a natural and cultural treasure.

In the early part of the 1900s research and studies of the native dog took place and for the first time the Japanese named dog breeds. Up until then dogs were just called Inu, meaning dog. The new breed names were mainly the name of the area the dogs originally came from. Hokkaido Ken, or Ainu Ken, were named after Hokkaido, the northern island. These were the medium-sized dogs mainly used for bear and deer hunting by the Ainu people. Akita Ken, the larger dog, was named after the Akita prefecture in the northern part of the main island. The Kishu Ken is a medium-size dog that is now white in colour, though he used to have colour. The Kishu Ken came from the Kishu and Mie prefectures in the south-western part of the main island and is used for boar and deer hunting. The Shikoku Inu is also medium-sized and was named after the south-western island. The Kishu and Shikoku are the most popular medium-sized dogs native to Japan today. There are several others including the Kai Ken, the Karafuto Ken and the Etsu no Inu.

ORIGIN OF THE SHIBA NAME

The only exception to the location rule is the Shiba Inu. Many stories of how the Shiba came by its name prevail. Small-size dogs around the Nagano prefecture in the central mountain areas of the Japanese mainland have been called Shiba Inu since time immemorial. You will hear the Shiba called the little Brushwood dog. This is because of his red colour and the speed with which he moves through the brush (brush is "shiba" in Japanese) when he is hunting. The Japanese also call small things, such as plant seeds, "shiba". It is important to understand that there are numerous characters with two or more meanings in the written Japanese language.

The Shibas from different regions were known by their regional names; for example the Shinshu Shiba came from the Shinshu area in Nagano prefecture, which is the central mountainous area of the mainland. The Gifu prefecture near Nagano produced the Mino Shiba, and

The Shiba is a superb hunting dog.

the Sanin Shiba came from the north-western part of the mainland.

THE SHIBA TRADITION

Shibas are superb hunting dogs, having lived in the mountainous regions. They are sure-footed, alert, quick and nimble. Fatigue is almost unknown to them. They were used to hunt any game from rabbits to deer in spite of their small size. They were also used to flush out birds. The Shibas skill in hunting is highlighted by the story of a man in the Wakayama Prefecture who said that he had captured twenty-seven deer in one season without a gun but solely with the help of a 'Shiba dog'. When you remember that hunting the deer in Japan is only allowed from the first of December to the end of the following February, this is truly a remarkable feat.

Shibas are loyal and trustworthy companions, and excellent watch dogs. The dogs living in the mountains were larger-boned and rougher-looking than the Shiba you know today. They are a very hardy dog, able to stand extreme temperatures of cold without kennelling.

There is a saying in Japan that "the dog will not forget the man who keeps him for three days." They believe that the Shiba likes cleanliness and will never enter its master's house. Although the Shiba will stay loyal to a master who feeds him and cares for him, he still remains independent and self-reliant and prefers to choose his own habitat.

Another story which portrays the Shiba's courage is that of the Regent Hideyoshi, who used to feed his favourite tiger a dog every day. One day a black and white dog was thrown into the cage. Against everyone's expectations it furiously sprang at the tiger's throat and would not let go. Though torn by the tiger's claws, it held on till they both died. Hideyoshi thought this was strange and demanded to know who had owned the dog. The dog's master was a man of Yamada, Tango Province; he and his wife had loved the dog dearly. The dog had been devoted to his master, accompanying him on his hunting expeditions every day. The village headman became jealous of the dog and had ordered it to be given to the Regent. The dog's master, indignant at the headman's plot, had taught it to kill the enemy first and then die. When the Regent was told of the plot, the headman was punished and his property was given to the poor couple to console their grief for the dog.

CULTURAL RECOGNITION

In the 1920s the Japanese people were becoming more aware of their heritage and culture. One such person was Dr H. Saito, who travelled all over Japan researching and studying the native dogs. He was given a great deal of co-operation from local people. It was on his advice that the different dog breeds were given the names which have been mentioned earlier.

In 1928 Dr Saito and fellow enthusiasts decided to form a Club. Four years later this Club became a government-sanctioned organisation for the preservation of the native dog and was called Nihon Ken Hozonkai (Nippo for short). The name means The Japanese Dog Preservation Society. The Shiba Inu and the Akita Ken were among the six original breeds to be identified. Then came the formation of the Society for the Preservation of the Nippon Inu.

Subsequently the Shiba Inu were brought down from the mountains to fanciers in the towns. The recognition of the Shiba Inu in 1936, and their designation as a 'precious natural resource' of Japan under the Cultural Properties Act, brought them recognition by the Fédération Cynologique Internationale (FCI) and registration with the Japanese Kennel Club (JKC) and with Nippo. The Shibas shown in Tokyo in the 1930s came from the Yamanashi or San In areas of Japan.

A Shiba male called Ishi, born in the San-in area, moved to Tokyo and was sold to Mr Takeo Sato. At the Nippo Headquarters show in 1936 he won a major award. Ishi was seen by a Mr Horiuchi of Shikoku, who was very impressed. Mr Horiuchi owned a female black and tan Shiba called Koro. She also did well in the show ring. When she was

The Japanese recognised the Shiba Inu as 'a precious natural resource'.

three she was mated to Ishi, who was then eight years old. Two puppies resulted – Aka-go and Ishi-go.

Aka-go was to be the first really important Shiba show dog and sire. As his show career progressed so did his prowess as a sire, culminating in some 200 litters being sired by him. One of his most influential offspring was a bitch called Beniko. She was mated to a male named Akani which produced the link in the chain of important foundation Shibas, a red male named Naka-go

Akaishiso, Akaishiso being the kennel name. Naka was the first Shiba to win a top award, namely the Nippo Trophy, which is the equivalent today of winning the Prime Minister's award. His show career was great but as a producer he was even better, siring five winners of the Prime Minister's award. Naka lived to the age of sixteen.

THE SIX ORIGINAL BREEDS
The six original breeds are as follows. The Akita is the largest of the Japanese Spitz breeds and was named after the prefecture in Northern Japan. This breed is centuries old and was developed originally as a fighting dog. The Akita was later used for hunting deer, bear and wild boar. The Akita is a fearless hunter. He is an excellent guard dog and a loyal and affectionate companion. He stands 24 to 28 inches at the withers and weighs around 75 to 100 pounds.

Then there are the medium-sized dogs in the Inu Group. The Kishu is from the mountainous area of Wakayama and Mie. As hunters, they originally accompanied the boar hunt. They were also used for herding and for guarding. Their colour is usually white which makes them stand out from their quarry. The Kishu stands around 17 to 22 inches.

The Shikoku is from the island of Shikoku. Little headway had been made in this breed until the 1930s. Mr Haruo Isogai took an interest in Japan's native breeds. The wealthy people in the city of Asaka used the Shikoku for their sport of deer hunting. Later the Shikoku became a companion guard dog. He stands 17 to 22 inches high and can be white, fawn, tan, grey and pied. The white and the tans are the most common colours.

The Kai came mainly from the Yamanashi prefecture of the central mainland of Japan. He was used for hunting deer. He is sometimes called a deer hound. He stands 18 to 23.5 inches high and weighs between 35 and 50 pounds. The Kai is always brindle, and his colours can be of red, black and grey. He is often known as the 'Tiger dog'.

The Hokkaido or Ainu came from the northern island of Hokkaido. These dogs were used for bear and deer hunting by the Ainu tribe in Japan. They are strong, fearless and courageous and will take on an opponent regardless of size. They

The Japanese Shiba Inu – the smallest of the six original breeds.

stand 18 to 22 inches high and weigh 45 to 66 pounds. Like the tribal people they accompanied, the Ainu have a sharp and ferocious temperament. The Japanese consider them to be one of the most versatile working breeds. Their colour is red.

And, of course, the smallest of the six original breeds is the Japanese Shiba Inu.

SAVED FROM EXTINCTION

Twice during its long history the Shiba faced extinction – once following World War II when all the Japanese breeds were decimated, and again in 1959 when a devastating epidemic of distemper broke out. Three founders of Nippo were given the special and difficult job of searching out the pure-bred specimens of the Shiba breed. Mr Masuezo Ozaki studied the Sanin Shiba, Mr Tatsuo Nakajo's interest was the Shinshu Shiba and Mr Gaiyu Ishikawa was identified with the Mino Shiba. The Mino Shiba was found to be mixed with the Mikawa Inu which, though it looked like a Shiba, had a restless and timid character. Its eyes were big and round and the body was brown with no white underneath.

Today's Shibas owe their existence to the careful breeding of the remaining dogs from the various regions. Many lines had only a few dogs left after the devastation, so they were introduced to each other to re-establish and preserve the qualities inherent in the dogs native to the region. This also accounts for the variation in Shiba type.

The Shinshu Shiba comes from the Nagano Prefecture, known as the 'Mecca' for the breed, probably because history claims this to be the region that originated the Shiba. The Sanin Shiba is from Yamanashi and Sanin area. At the point of extinction the Shinshu and Sanin were carefully bred to preserve the type. The Mino Shiba was also brought back from extinction by the Shinshu Line, so is similar in type.

The lines have merged to produce, in varying degrees, a dog which is highly intelligent, with keen senses, which is strong in body, tireless in movement, and fearless in stature, wrapped up in the most attractive package that we call the Shiba Inu.

GETTING ORGANISED

Nippo organised its first dog show in Tokyo in 1928. This show was equivalent to that of today's Nippo National show. The first prize winner and winner of the Prime Minister's award was a Hokkaido Ken named Goro-go. The breed standard was established in 1934. The present Nippo standard has been revised twice since then. The show encouraged Japanese dog fanciers and was continued yearly from then until 1942. The medium-sized dogs, Hokkaido Ken, Kishu Ken, and Shikoku Ken, were always the winners of the first prizes, with the exception of the last show held just before World War II when a large-sized dog won the prize. He was a Hayabusa-go.

With the organisation of the Nippo shows many native dogs were moved from the mountain areas to the cities, where planned breeding programmes were set up. The serious breeders also imported Shibas from other areas of the country to improve the quality according to the Standard.

With the coming of war, Japan's economy, especially with regards to the food situation, was bad and it meant that many breeders had to give up their dogs. Mr Ozaki was fortunate to be given a special food allowance by the local government to keep his Shibas. But the effect of the war, as I have said earlier, just when Japan's preservation efforts had begun to take effect, devastated Nippo's efforts to preserve the native dog. After the war Nippo held its first show in the spring of 1949. It was a memorable show for the Shiba, for it was a Shiba called Naka-go that took the first prize, thus achieving the top honour for the first time.

At this time the Akita was the most popular native dog. Many American servicemen and civilians who were stationed in Japan bought them and took them back to the States on their return there. The big dog also became the Japanese *nouveau riche* status symbol. The most popular Akita was 'Kongo-go', then 'Goromaru-go' and later 'Tamakumo-go'. These are all Akita names for dogs. But in time, and with the critics against the Akita Ken, plus social demands for a smaller type of dog, the Akita's popularity declined. Thus, today, the most popular native dog is the Shiba Inu.

THE NIPPO NATIONAL SHOWS
Nippo celebrated its 60th anniversary on September 4th, 1988 with more than 20,000 members. Nippo now holds two National shows a year, in the Spring and in the Autumn, as well as 40 regional and local shows that are also held twice a year. The main purpose of the shows is not competition but evaluation.

Nearly 40,000 Shibas are registered annually in Japan, ranking the Shiba as the most popular native dog in Japan. At the National Show held in November 1996 the entry drew 711 top-ranked Shibas. The medium-sized dogs and the small-sized dogs only compete against each other finally for the Best in Show (Prime Minister's Award and Nippo Prize).

Males and females compete individually. They also compete within their different age groups in their own classes, thus being evaluated against their own sex and within their own age group. The dogs are judged twice; individually in the morning and as a group in the afternoon. In the morning before judging starts the dog has his teeth checked and counted by the assistant judge.

The judge makes notes on each dog's judging sheet. He will then tell the handler to move the dog, at a trot, in front of him, to see the dog's movement. The judge does not touch the dog at any time. If the dog has good inborn structure he should stand firm by himself. In the afternoon the dogs enter the ring in the judge's order

The dogs are judged "A" Yuryo = Excellent, "B" Tokuryo= Very Good, or "C" Ryo = Good or they are left unmarked. The results are published in a monthly magazine with judges' comments only about the top class dogs. There is no points system for Champions in Japan. In Japan the Shibas are very standardised now and at shows they are very difficult to differentiate one from another. They are very much the same size and same type. The most important judging point is their character, more so than their outward appearance.

2 *CHOOSING A SHIBA INU*

The Shiba is one of the Spitz Group of dogs. Though small in stature he stands out in a crowd. His brilliant colour, fur-like coat and strong, sturdy body are only surpassed by his wonderful head and alert expression which comes from those dark almond pools, his eyes. Look into those eyes and you are lost forever. From the tip of his pricked ears to the end of his lush curled tail he oozes confidence and nobility – a dog which proclaims that he is second to none. His fox-like appearance is eye-catching.

The Shiba is cat-like in many of his ways. He will preen himself constantly, checking his nails and grooming his coat. As a breed they are totally odourless and are extremely clean and fastidious. They love to laze in the sunshine. They play catch and chase toys, standing on their back legs and pawing with their front legs, stalking through the grass and climbing and jumping where and when their explorations make it necessary. They are wonderful, loyal companions.

The Shiba is a very basic, close-to-nature animal, confident and loyal to the hand that feeds him, cautious and wary of strangers. He is strong in his territorial domination. His natural instincts are to be the Alpha dog – leader of the pack. He will challenge other males and defend his rights, regardless of the size of his opponent. Shibas are highly intelligent and quick to learn, but can be incredibly stubborn when they want to be. It is essential that training is begun at the earliest opportunity; six weeks of age would not be too soon.

The hunting instinct in the Shiba is paramount. When off the lead, should a bird flush up from the undergrowth, he will be gone into the blue yonder, totally oblivious of everything and everybody until the quarry is either caught or has disappeared. Shibas have a great aptitude for surviving for days, weeks and months in the wild! This is a very independent and capable dog. It is true to say that you never truly own a Shiba, they own you. But when he gives you that unique Shiba grin you know you've cracked it!

ESSENCE AND EXPRESSION
The Japanese are very specific and set

ESSENCE AND EXPRESSION
Photos: John Daniels.

LEFT: The Shiba encapsulates spirited boldness.   *RIGHT: Brave without being foolhardy.*

great store by 'Essence and its Expression' when defining the Shiba Inu. We would use the word 'Temperament' for this definition. In the Japanese Standard it is valued at 15 per cent of the total score when judging the Shiba. In broad terms 'temperament' means personality and the nature of the dog, that is, its Essence, and how the dog expresses and reflects its nature to the world – its Expression. The dog has a spirited boldness with a good nature and a feeling of artlessness. It is alert and able to move quickly with nimble, elastic steps.

The Japanese have words which describe both physical and mental traits in the Shiba. 'Kan-i' translates as 'spirited boldness', a very important characteristic of the Japanese dog. The Japanese word

'Kikaku' (spirited) implies bravery, calmness, boldness and alertness but also obedience. To have Kan-i, in other words, means to be brave without being foolhardy. Be bold, but be alert to danger and be at all times under the control of the master.

'Ryosei' literally translates as 'good-natured'. From a dog that has Ryosei you will have a gentle disposition – he will be faithful and obedient but will also possess a good watchdog and companion-dog attitude. With these attributes he needs to have intelligence, so it is of the utmost importance to the Japanese dog that he is astute as well as having good habits and a calm nature. Being of a good nature and responding quickly to the commands of his master does not mean that he is cowardly, for

16

The Shiba 'smile'

Astute, yet calm.

sometimes his quick response to a command might require him to have fighting spirit and courage, which he must obey instantly and fearlessly. Thus, on reflection, Kan-i and Ryosei are two sides of the same coin. For the dog with correct Kan-i will have correct Ryosei, as one cannot exist without the other.

'Soboku' is modesty and gentleness but also means having the ability to project character and grace. The refinement and flavour of dignity is said to be the very marrow of Soboku. The Japanese consider that possessing all of these traits is absolutely vital in producing the 'Essence' in the Japanese dog. In the later chapter on the show dog you will again see where these traits of the Shiba are essential requirements.

RESPONSIBILITIES OF OWNERSHIP

Now that you understand the Shiba character you need to ask yourself several questions before becoming a Shiba owner. Are you the right person to own a dog? If so, is a Shiba the right dog for you and your immediate family? There is no doubt that they are an appealing and beautiful breed. Their attractive looks are what first catches your eye. They seem to stand out in a crowd. They are confident and self-assured and full of their own importance. Though small, they are quick and agile and have an alert demeanour. Ask yourself if you have the time and the patience to occupy and stimulate this brain. Are you physically up to the Shiba and, more important, is your family up to it? Does anyone suffer with allergies that could be aggravated by the fur-like coat that the Shiba has?

Remember you are taking on a responsibility that needs feeding, housing and health care for many years to come, for the Shiba can live to a ripe old age, to sixteen or eighteen years old. So you can see that they are a long-term commitment. Are the other members of your family up to a lively, boisterous companion sharing their environment? Have you an elderly family member that might have difficulty manoeuvring around a sprightly youngster, who is liable to bump into them?

Is your garden secure and are the fences and walls sufficiently high to stop the Shiba scaling them? In the beginning you need to be home with the new puppy, for he has to be fed and exercised frequently and his training must start from day one in his new home. If you work, it is better to wait until you are able to be home with him. If you make the wrong decision about having a dog, and it ends up with the dog having to be re-homed, this is traumatic for both of you, and unnecessary. So take a long hard look at your family circumstances.

If you have small children you need to be extra vigilant for their sakes as well as the puppy's. Young children can be rough and can tease without meaning to be unkind. This must be considered and handled accordingly. Many Shibas are brought up with children and the two co-exist without any problems but it is something you must consider. Only you know how your children behave.

If, having considered all these points, you decide that a Shiba is for you, it is important to gather as much information on the breed as possible. You will need to spend time visiting shows and talking to breeders and exhibitors before you decide from whom you will purchase your Shiba.

FINDING YOUR FAVOURITE TYPE
Your national Kennel Club will be only too happy to help you. You will be able to get names of the breeders of Shibas close to you and find out where puppies are available. You can also obtain details of shows to visit so that you will be able to see the Shiba in numbers. The various Shiba Inu Clubs can also be contacted for this information.

Most breeders will give you the third degree and ask the questions I have already raised. It is done with the best of intentions, for they know only too well that the wrong dog in the wrong home causes much heartache for all concerned. Breeders want only the best for their puppies, having planned their breeding, watched their whelping and nurtured them towards leaving the nest and joining a new family. It is important to them to be sure that every puppy is going to a good home, and a permanent home for life.

Having seen the Shibas at shows you will quickly become aware of the different types. This should not be so, but it is a fact of life. People's interpretation of the Standard varies. Different bloodlines produce variation in type, and you must first decide what you prefer and what you consider closest fits the Standard and which you wish to own. Check out the pedigrees of these dogs and see if they come from the same breeding. This should indicate whether they are 'common' to the breeder of your choice. There may be several breeders breeding the same lines, or similar bloodlines, and this will then give you an excellent chance of choosing a puppy.

Your puppy should be a good example of the type coming from that kennel and should mature into the type of Shiba that you have seen and admired in the show ring. Breeders who have bred for a number of years become known for a type – they seem to stamp their ideals on the dogs they breed. If this is the type you are looking for, you can usually be sure that the puppy will grow up looking like the other stock from that kennel. When visiting the breeder ask to see photos of past and present dogs so that you can check back on the ancestors of your future puppy. Ask about any hereditary problems that the breeder may have experienced.

ASSESSING A BREEDER

How does the breeder relate to her dogs? Do the dogs seem happy and contented? What sort of condition are the elderly dogs in – are they still special to her and do they still have a zest for life? Are the kennels clean and comfortable? Do the dogs have plenty of exercise areas? How do they react to strangers? It is important to be able to meet and handle some of the dogs face to face. If you are going to share your home with one, it is good to know how it acts on its home territory. While the show ring shows you how well he is trained, how beautiful he is and how sociable he can be, it is a false atmosphere, and the Shiba knows this, for he is a great actor and character player.

You need to see him at play and in the company of other dogs. While the Shiba

is, at first, usually a little aloof and stand-offish, once he has gained confidence and has accepted you in his home territory he should approach you gradually and allow you to pet him. He should not be frightened or nervous and disappear to the other end of the house or garden, for this could indicate that his temperament is not all it should be.

Do ask as many questions as you feel are necessary; the breeder will be happy to satisfy you on all aspect of the Shiba. And, I repeat, the good breeder will ask you many questions about yourself. Do you work? What is your home environment, and what are your expectations and future plans for the pup? How much do you know of the breed? Have you owned dogs before and what happened to them? Breeders want what is best for their Shiba puppies and only by questioning you can they determine and satisfy their requirements on the puppy's behalf .

It is wise after having visited the kennels to give yourselves some breathing and thinking space before contacting the breeder and booking your pup. Be wary of the breeder "that just happens to have a pup you can take today!" Ask yourself *why*? Good stock usually has to be booked in advance. Once you have booked your puppy you must sit back and wait for his, or her, arrival.

DOG OR BITCH?

You will know that Shibas are from the Spitz group of dogs, which means that in common with most Spitz-type dogs they have a mind of their own. They can be loving and affectionate but still retain aloofness. They have a quick keen brain which needs plenty of stimulation and they need lots of people contact. Left to their own devices they make everything an adventure! And, as already mentioned, they are very dominant, so, firstly, you have to consider whether your puppy is to be a dog or a bitch?

The male in most breeds is larger and more impressive. With the Shiba there is not a great deal of size difference between the sexes. The male does have a stronger head than the female. He also has an arrogance and an aura! The male's assertiveness is something that you must consider. However, both sexes can be aloof with strangers.

If you already have a dog, is it a male? Is he assertive and how is he going to react to the Shiba. Remember that the Shiba is good with dogs larger than himself but will dominate anything the same size or smaller. With larger dogs he will show some respect – provided, of course, he is given respect! This applies to both the male and females. He will also try to dominate you, so be sure to set down the rules of co-existence early on. This breed thinks, which is a great quality, and can be channelled to your advantage. The Shiba is not a dog to be taken lightly. It is not an 'easy' breed to own – though beautiful to look at, he has not been told he is a small dog and he doesn't behave like one. A lap-dog he is not!

The females are slightly smaller and more feminine but remember they carry a number of the same traits as the male and can be equally independent. Her style, beauty and her strength of character are priceless, for she also holds the key to the future of the breed and she is capable of producing one of those impressive males. While you can have the services of the best male in the country, you are unlikely to be able to buy the best bitch. The bitch is precious: while the male often outshines the female, she is the way to the future. Remember that Shiba females can have two seasons a year and quite often have their first season as early as five months of age. Sexual activity can go on indefinitely. If you have no desire to breed your Shiba, then having her spayed after her first season is usually recommended. All Shibas shed their coats profusely twice a year; the females usually prior to a season and also when they have had a litter. Whether male or female, the Shiba will love its family and be steadfast and loyal to its keeper.

PET OR SHOW DOG?
The next point to consider is whether the new puppy is to be a family pet – or have you aspirations to show him? Whatever, it is important to be clear in your own mind initially – then be honest and clear with the breeder that you have decided to buy your puppy from. With the best will in the world, breeders are not psychic; they can only advise from their experience of the breed and how they have seen previous puppies, born from a similar mating, progress. It is important to have seen both the mother and the father of your future pup so you can gauge their temperament, size and overall type. It is important that the sire, dam and the litter are Kennel Club registered.

VISITING THE LITTER
The first time you see a litter of Shiba puppies (which should be at around six

The puppy will change dramatically in the first few weeks of life. This three-week-old puppy appears to be sesame in colour.

Within three weeks, the puppy has become red.

ASSESSING A PUPPY
Photos: John Daniels.

ABOVE: Temperament is all-important, and the puppy should be bright and alert.

RIGHT: A small, sturdy, well-balanced puppy of Spitz type.

The head appears as a blunt triangle.

*One ear may go up before the other
– it is nothing to worry about.*

The nose is jet-black.

*The almond-shaped eyes
are dark-brown in colour.*

White markings on the face, chest and underparts of the body visible at six weeks.

The black mask will fade by the time the dog reaches maturity.

LEFT: Stepping out with excellent forehand reach.

RIGHT: Light and energetic movement.

*The puppy will feel
bewildered when he
first arrives in his
new home.*

weeks of age) you will be amazed at how much like an adult dog they are. They have that arrogance and confident appearance that is truly Shiba. Providing they have had a good start in life, they will all look cuddly and appealing but remember – it is all down to their genes: they will inherit the good points as well as the bad points from their parents, though they are not necessarily apparent at this moment. This is why it is important that you see both parents, if at all possible. Sometimes you might have to travel to see the sire elsewhere if he is owned by another breeder, which is often the case. The puppies will also inherit characteristics from their grandparents. It is good to watch the puppies at play and to see how they interact with the other dogs. You will see differences that are apparent even at this early age.

When the day arrives to go and visit your future puppy, wear sensible clothes, preferably trousers. If you are taking young children, trousers are a must for

them, for puppies will jump up and their little claws can scratch quite badly and this could make for a bad first experience for the child – and also the puppies, who will get screeched at. You will find you also spend most of your time sitting on the floor playing with the little darlings. A child should always go down to ground level with puppies rather than try to pick them up, for a wriggling, squirming puppy can easily drop out of a child's arms and be injured.

Usually puppies fly in from all corners when visitors come to see them. Beware of the puppy that sits back and does not want to be part of the melee or goes off on his own. He is not the one for you, especially if you have small children. He needs to be placed, perhaps, with older people who lead a quieter life-style where his biggest contribution will be to sit on the sofa alongside them and be continually fussed, perhaps even a one-to-one situation where someone is living on their own and the dog will be the centre of his or her world.

This should not be the time you are taking your puppy home. The first visit is to see the puppies and be really sure about owning a Shiba, remembering you are making a long-term commitment. If the breeder is allowing you to choose your puppy, then you should spend as much time as possible watching their antics and assessing their dispositions in relation to you and your family's expectations. Personally, I feel that the breeder is the best person to select a puppy for new owners, especially if it is the first Shiba you have owned, for she has spent every day since their birth, watching them and seeing how they have developed their individual characters.

You may find that the breeder is unhappy for you to handle the puppies; if so, respect her wishes, for she has their well-being at heart and is ever-conscious of the possibility of infection being passed on to them. Most breeders have a constant stream of visitors and prospective new puppy-owners when they have a litter for sale, and until the puppies are ready to leave and go to their respective new homes, their health and safety is the breeder's main concern. Puppies are usually ready to leave the nest at around eight to ten weeks but again this is very much dependent on the breeder.

THE FINAL CHOICE

When choosing your pup you will need to observe the litter, particularly if you are looking for a dog with show potential. Usually one puppy will stand out from the rest. Check that he is not spoken for already. Watch his stance and movement as well as the puppy's overall appearance. Having read up on the Standard of the Shiba you will know how important it is that any markings that he has are correct and, most important, that he has a correct bite, even though at this time they are still his milk teeth. Look at the shape of his head: are his ears up? What about the set of his tail? Is he strong on his legs? Does he move freely?

If you have any doubts about your puppy, raise them with the breeder. If they are conscientious they will answer your question openly and honestly; they will want you to be sure and happy with the pup. If you are unsure, then think again. Many breeders will be only too happy to explain the differences between the pups, as they see them. Remember they are watching and observing the litter all the time.

New owners have their 'ideal' dog in mind but sometimes, seeing all the puppies together, they lose sight of this and fall for something totally different. A good breeder will be able to match up the right owner with the right pup for the right reasons! If for any reason you are not happy with the puppies you see, do not be afraid to say so. Remember there is likely to be another litter available in the near future, and it is better to wait if you are unsure and, again, a good breeder will understand this.

PREPARING FOR THE PUPPY

Once all your questions have been answered and you have chosen your puppy, you will need to have made preparations before going back to collect him. Shibas being the Houdinis of the dog world, your garden will need to be well-fenced and secure. Latches and handles can be easily flicked open with a little practice! And a six-foot fence holds no great challenge to a determined Shiba .

A vari-crate is a must. This is a plastic box with a door on the front and air vents all round. Place a square of vet-bed for him to lie on inside. It gives the puppy his own place to go into and sleep and you have somewhere to confine him when necessary. It needs to be about 50cm (20ins) high and 60cm (24ins) long. It will also help you to toilet-train your pup – more of that later. You will need a feeding dish and a chrome water dish, a collar and lead for street walking and a Flexi lead for those country walks, a wire brush and a metal comb.

If you are to kennel him outside it is important that his kennel is close to the house and that he has a wired-in run. He needs to be in close contact with his family and the day-to-day routines of the house. If possible, a dog-flap from the house into his kennel and run would be ideal, thus giving him freedom to join the family as and when he wants, when they are around, but also giving him his own secure space when he wants it.

DOCUMENTATION
Before you leave with your puppy the breeder should give you his pedigree form and his registration documentation. The Pedigree form is a list of his ancestors behind his sire and dam and this is made out by the breeder on a blank form. It will have his name, date of birth, his breed and his sex, the name of his sire and dam and the breeder's name and address. If your puppy has pure-bred Champions in his ancestry, the pedigree

reflects this and is valuable evidence of his good breeding. But sometimes the names on the pedigree are meaningless, as is the paper itself. Just because a dog has a pedigree it does not necessarily mean he has been registered at the Kennel Club.

The Registration document is issued by the Kennel Club and verifies that your puppy's parents were pure-bred dogs of the breed your puppy represents. It will have the puppy's registered name on it, his date of birth and his sex, and will, at this stage, be registered in the name of the breeder. You will need to re-register the puppy in your name and address at the Kennel Club as his new owners. He must be Kennel Club registered if you wish to show him and use him in a breeding programme at a later date.

The breeder will also give you a daily feeding chart which you should observe closely to start with. It is important to keep the puppy on the same diet when you first take him home, certainly for the first month. Modifying it later must be done gradually over a period of a week or more.

The breeder should also give you vaccination documents if the puppy has already received any injections. You show this to the vet of your choice when you take your newly-acquired puppy along for his check-up and further vaccinations.

THE FIRST FEW DAYS
You should have someone accompany you when you collect the pup. It is important that his first car journey is a pleasant experience not a scary one. The back seat of the car should be covered with a blanket just in case the puppy is sick; a towel is also useful. Your

companion should sit with the puppy in the back and have him either on their lap or by their side, giving the puppy encouragement throughout the journey. Most Shibas love the car and are only too ready to jump in the moment the door is opened.

When you arrive home remember that everything will be strange to the pup. The journey will have been quite tiring for him, so give him time to collect himself and explore his new surroundings. He will, no doubt, want to relieve himself so, unless the area is totally secure, put him onto a collar and lead before taking him into the garden. Take him to the part of the garden that you are happy for him to use for his toilet training; if you do this regularly he will soon get the message.

Apart from your immediate family in the house, it is a good idea to give the puppy a few days to settle in before outside friends and family come to visit him, and remember that he is not complete with his health checks and injections, so caution to begin with is wise.

Puppies quite often go off their food for a day or so when they go into new homes and a different environment. It is important to say at this point that Shibas are not food-oriented like most breeds. They amaze me how little they really eat. They are quite nocturnal and I have found that a bowl of food left by them at night is usually gone in the morning. Whatever you do, don't panic if he is a bit off his food at first. Do not be tempted to feed him treats from your table, for this can become a habit. So do not start it. If in doubt, ring the breeder.

The first night in his new home is quite stressful for him. Remember that up till now he has been one of several puppies, and Mum has been there, and there has been someone to cuddle up to. Last thing at night take him out in the garden *on a lead* to spend a penny. Return him to his crate or kennel and settle him down and leave him. For sure he will whine for a while, but steel yourself against it. Plug your ears if necessary but do not be tempted to go down and take him back to bed with you. It is fatal to do that, for then he will learn very quickly that all he has to do is whine for attention.

Before picking up the puppy you will have made arrangements with your local veterinary surgery to take the puppy along for a health check and, if required, his vaccinations, having checked first what, if any, vaccinations he has had at the breeder's premises. This initial visit to the vet should be about three days after you have collected him from the breeder. It is important to give the puppy time to get to know you and your home and gain a bit of confidence from this. His visit to the surgery should be as free from stress as possible. He needs you to be calm and reassuring throughout his visit. Carry the puppy from the car into the waiting room and keep him in your arms until you go into the see the vet. Place him gently on the table and cuddle and reassure him the whole time you are with the vet. An initial bad experience at the vet's has ruined many an otherwise stable dog. Once the puppy has had all his injections the vet will tell you when it is safe to take him out in public places for his walks.

3 CARING FOR YOUR SHIBA INU

Shibas are not the best feeders in the world. They can be finicky and difficult. Perhaps because they are still fairly primeval, they retain an inborn desire to feed and forage when they feel the need, and not necessarily when we feel they should eat. As I mentioned before, they are very nocturnal and quite often will feed through the night as opposed to through the day. They seem able to go several days without eating and to suffer no undue effects.

DIET
The Shiba seems to favour cooked chicken and rice, brown preferably, a diet which is understandable when one considers their ancestry. With numerous well-known and well-trusted brand names on the market who produce a chicken and rice, or lamb and rice combination, this should make feeding easier. But, just when you think you have found the one he likes, your Shiba will take an about turn and stop eating it! Boiled fish is another good protein commodity that he will accept and enjoy for a while. Likewise, cooked turkey or

rabbit can tempt them to eat. Some owners have found that the Shiba does well on green tripe.

When cooking the family's meal, cook a little extra vegetable and mix it in with the Shiba's food. A little grated raw carrot on his meal will also be acceptable to him occasionally. Strangely enough, their inability to be motivated by food rarely seems to have any outward ill-effects. Whatever they manage to eat seems to be well utilised within them for maximum effect.

Your Shiba should be fed twice a day once he is past six months of age, morning and evening. Up until six months he should be fed at least three times a day. If he is not eating as well as you would like, refrain from feeding him anything between meals so that he is ready for his meal when it is put down for him.

Our feeding programme for the day is exercise followed by a meal in the morning (usually between 6:00 and 9:00 am) and exercise followed by his meal in the evening.(between 5:00 and 7:00 pm), with a final exercise before bedding

Tronkaer Yoko Suko pictured at eight weeks old: During the growing period, it is essential that the Shiba is given a top-quality, balanced diet.

Photo: Kirsten Jorgensen.

Tronkaer Yoko Suko at nine months of age showing excellent balance and bone development.

Photo: Kirsten Jorgensen.

down. I never feed milk to dogs once they have been weaned from the mother. I have found that it inevitably makes their motions loose. A bowl of water is always available and changed frequently.

WEIGHT WATCHING
Shibas seem to put on weight very easily and it is essential to watch their weight gain. Carrying too much weight is detrimental: as with humans, it puts unnecessary strain on the heart. Shibas

If you have more than one dog, they will exercise themselves through play.

Photo: Amy Campbell.

kept outside in kennels seem to eat better than those living in the house. They are, of course, more active in a kennel and run and perhaps need more fuel inside them to keep warm. It is not good to have to change diets too frequently, though an occasional change can be beneficial. When changing a diet it should be done gradually over three or four days to give the gut a chance to assimilate the new food. If your Shiba is happy and content on a particular diet then continue to feed him on it. Feeling that he might become bored with the same old diet is in your mind, *not* his.

EXERCISE
The Shiba needs quite a bit of exercise. If you have two Shibas together they automatically exercise each other through play. Though the Shiba is very lively throughout the day, he still seems to need a free-running period. While most people are reluctant to let the Shiba off lead for fear of his not returning, even the best-trained Shiba in recall will turn a

The Shiba requires a period of free-running every day.

deaf ear if a bird flushes out of the undergrowth to take his attention.

I bike my dogs daily – not loose, I hasten to add, having bought a bike harnessing attachment on one of my visits abroad. The dog is tethered on one side of the bike to a spring-loaded arm. He is then able to run safely and securely alongside without hampering the cyclist, whose hands are free to manoeuvre the bike. Lead-walking is also an essential part of his exercise and control. Each day you should have a play time with your Shiba, preferably individually if you have more than one. This special time is very important to you both: it is your time to check on conditioning and focus, and his time to open up his character to you.

GROOMING
Grooming should be a pleasurable time for both you and your Shiba. It is your special time together away from other dogs and any other distractions. It should become something your Shiba looks forward to on a daily basis. The Shiba's coat sheds dirt easily and does not matt unless he is badly neglected. Shibas, being the hardy and resilient little dogs that they are, do not need the pampering and grooming that many other breeds require. A daily brushing

GROOMING
Photos: John Daniels.

Grooming should start at an early age. The puppy will soon learn to relax and enjoy the attention.

will remove the dead hair and keep the skin clean. Bathing the Shiba is more a case of choice then necessity, for the Shiba is a particularly clean and fastidious dog, more cat-like than dog-like in this respect. They are totally odourless and are constantly cleaning and preening themselves.

The Shiba, in common with other Spitz breeds, has a double coat. The undercoat is soft and dense, which is his insulation, while the top coat is harsh and straight and is used to keep out the dirt and the weather. The Shiba male will shed his undercoat twice a year, normally in spring and autumn. The female Shiba will also shed undercoat after a litter of puppies.

NAIL CARE
Nails should be trimmed frequently if the dog is kept in the house and exercises only on grass, as they will grow quite rapidly. If you can exercise your Shiba on concrete surfaces this helps to keep the nails short. If nails have to be trimmed it is essential that this procedure is begun in puppyhood. Be sure to check the

dewclaws, for these grow long, curl round and catch on things. They can also cause damage to your Shiba.

Dogs in general hate their nails being clipped and Shibas, in particular, can be extremely unco-operative. It can take two people with a great deal of assertive effort to hold a Shiba still sufficiently long to clip his nails. The yells and squeals he emits have to be heard to be believed. I heard of a breeder that devised a method whereby she suspended her Shiba in a bag which contained a hole just big enough for one foot at a time to protrude through, which enabled her to clip her Shiba's nails on her own. I must admit I have never tried this myself. Take great care not to catch the quick of the nail, for this can be very painful – for both of you, if the Shiba decides to retaliate. You may need to muzzle the Shiba while you are nail-clipping.

As you have probably gathered, nail-clipping the Shiba is not for the faint-hearted. When picking up your puppy from his breeder, have a word with them about nail-clipping. They may well be

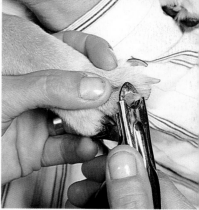

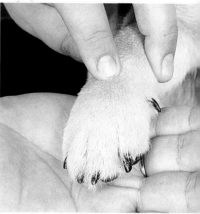

NAIL CARE
Photos: John Daniels.

ABOVE: You may need to muzzle your Shiba during nail-cutting.

TOP RIGHT: Care must be taken not to cut the nails too short.

RIGHT: The nails after clipping.

happy to show you how to do it and, initially, to clip them for you. There are numerous types of nail clippers on the market. If all else fails, filing them can be just as effective and, if done frequently from an early age, will keep the nails in good order. A fairly coarse emery board is sufficient.

USING A GROOMING TABLE
Using a grooming table makes the task of nail-cutting easier on your back and is a good training exercise for the Shiba. For just a few moments a day he has to acquiesce and be handled. He must learn to accept your attentions whether he likes it or not; so be firm, be kind, but be persistent – all very important if he is going to be shown.

Examining his teeth at these times also gets him used to the procedure for the show ring. At grooming time you can also check him over for ticks and fleas, paying careful attention to the base of the tail for any signs of bare patches. His ears should also be examined regularly for any secretions.

Using a grooming table also gets him used to being examined on a table at shows for, although in Japan the breed is always shown on the floor, most other countries see fit to show the Shiba on a table. The Shiba should never be trimmed out but should be shown in his natural state. This also applies to his whiskers, though some do trim off the whiskers. Good feeding is the basis of a good coat and good condition. Useful tools to have include a slicker brush, a steel rake or comb, a stiff bristle brush and nail clippers.

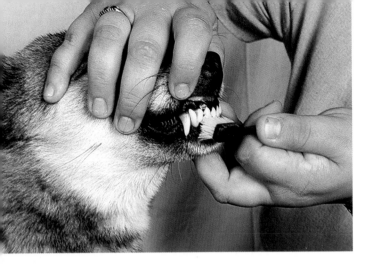

Teeth can be kept clean by regular brushing.

SHEDDING COAT

Bathing the Shiba should only be done when it is absolutely necessary. When the coat starts to loosen is a good time to bath your Shiba, for this gets rid of the loose hair and then makes it easier to groom out. Usually all the undercoat will come out, together with some of the top coat. What remains is a bedraggled, hairless-looking creature that bears no resemblance to your beautiful cuddly bear. From head to toe the transformation is dramatic. Gone are the lovely cheeks and plush ears. Gone is the bushy tail that counter-balances his outstanding head, and what is left in the middle could be mistaken for a stick insect. The Shiba seems to go totally out of condition at moulting time; he even sometimes loses what bit of appetite he has. This is all perfectly normal. Continue to feed as normal. Once the coat is right out it will take several weeks for it to return As the coat's new growth appears, the Shiba's appetite will improve. Grooming regularly once the new coat appears is important to attain that lovely plush appearance once again.

Shibas throw coat in different ways. Some shed their coat like a fleece: the undercoat lifts from the body and comes to the surface as a mass of dead fluff; it is lighter in colour and thick, dead and woolly in texture. This can then be lifted off the coat with a rake-type comb, leaving the top coat, though sparse, looking somewhat better in colour. If you are lucky, and can stand leaving the coat fleece till it goes down the full length of the Shiba, you can then remove the fleece in one or two grooming sessions. Other Shibas shed undercoat in patches; firstly you will notice the hair lifting on the back legs and you will just finish getting rid of this when they will start shedding coat on the shoulders, then on the side of the body, and so on, until all the undercoat has gone and then the re-growth appears.

You can expect your Shiba to take a few months to get back into peak condition. Throughout the moulting the Shiba seems to be totally unaware of his transformation – only you will be devastated, wondering if your beautiful creature will ever appear again, but rest assured he will, and the consolation is that the coat gets better and better both in texture and depth of colour. There are many products on the market that promise this and that for good coats, but remember there is nothing better for coat condition and overall dog health than a good diet.

34

TRAINING YOUR SHIBA

When the puppies were in the nest the breeder will have spent many hours playing and bonding with them. Though the majority of them will go on to their new owners, they will have been acclimatised to being handled, loved and caressed. They will have begun to bond and to trust their second mother, the breeder, accepting her and the conditions she imposes – albeit sometimes with reluctance. Placing them on their backs in the submissive position while rubbing their tummies and talking to them baby-like, is something they become accustomed to and enjoy. Holding the puppy up close to your face, nose to nose, and looking into his eyes while softly talking to him, makes him focus on you. Both of these exercises are training, though the puppy is not yet aware of it. It is important that by three months of age the Shiba puppy has been conditioned to trust and focus on you. Conditioning your Shiba prepares him and you for handling the undesirable behaviour common to the breed which may rear its head later in life. You will

Puppies in a litter tend to focus on each other.

When your puppy arrives home he must learn to look to his human pack leader
.

Photo: John Daniels.

Photo: John Daniels.

Puppies learn through play, and this can be a good time to teach some 'house rules'.

Photo: Ally Boughton.

then be able to avoid the bad behaviour or channel it, using it to your advantage.

The Shiba has an ability to turn off or go deaf on you. It may be something he seems to practise on you from time to time as he gets older. It is his way of testing you and determining just who is in control. He needs to know that you are as aware of this as he is and that if anything needs handling or sorting out, you are the one to do it, *not* him. It may be that you are out one day and another dog comes towards you who has shown your Shiba some aggression in the past. Your quick summing-up of the situation, and your immediate evasive actions to avoid trouble, become the pattern of behaviour that he expects from you. I always try to offset situations or pre-empt them. I never allow my dogs to get into a situation which they have to get out of by themselves. Aggression is a

dog's defence when he is put in an uncompromising position. Getting your dog's *total* attention on you at all times is something that you work on from puppyhood, and expand on as time goes by. Turning a deaf ear to you is not acceptable behaviour and the quicker your Shiba learns this, the better for all concerned. Eye dominance is an important part of this training.

Gaining your Shiba's trust, which is started in the nest with handling, caressing and loving, conditions him to trust you. Knowing you are there to protect him, come what may, in turn suppresses his self-preservation habit. Picking your puppy up, carrying him around on his back and confining him in your arms for short periods of time while he is very young teaches him that he must accept your restraints, and your attentions, even though he may want to resist.

Building up the length of time you restrain him should be done gradually. The puppy should be aware, and clear about what is expected of him, so you *must* be clear and precise in your instructions to him. If he is confused or unsure he will lose faith in you and revert to taking charge himself.

CHASTISING YOUR PUPPY
If you need to chastise puppy then always do it in the same way. Roll him over onto his back and, holding him down firmly, growl in his face, telling him what a naughty boy he is. Be sure to give him eye-contact and hold his gaze until you have finished reprimanding him. This is a dominance trait used by animals, so use it. It is amazing how quickly he will get the message. He then knows instantly that he has done something wrong, and what to expect. This is an ideal way of chastising him, for the Shiba never out-grows this form of control.

Once the puppy has understood that he has done wrong, then relax your grip on him, soften your voice, and tell him you still love him, and give him cuddles. He will then relax and will probably lick you, understanding that he is being

37

forgiven. Bawling and shouting at your dog achieves nothing, nor does it gain respect – and respect between you and your Shiba is the key to success.

TOILET TRAINING

Toilet training, as was mentioned earlier, is something that comes naturally to the Shiba. So long as you remember on waking, and after eating, always to take your Shiba outside to spend his pennies, he will be clean. He will usually stand by the door to go out, or whine to be let out, when he wishes to go to the toilet. When I have a young puppy in the house, if I am going out I will put him into his indoor kennel, knowing full well that he will not foul his sleeping area. On my return I immediately put him out into the garden for him to relieve himself. I am never disappointed. Lots of praise and encouragement should be given each time he conforms and performs. I have *never* had a dirty Shiba.

LEAD TRAINING

Lead training is another matter. Restrictions of any kind are not something the Shiba takes kindly to. But persistence, firmness, kindness and encouragement can move mountains –

and that is a Shiba if he digs his heels in. He should never be allowed to get away with *anything*, for he will capitalise on it. Shibas are survivors and they will turn most situations around to their way of thinking if given the opportunity.

Lead training should have begun at around five weeks. Check when you pick the puppy up from the breeder if this has been started – if not, then you begin the procedure yourself with the puppy. Start by putting on a collar for just a short period of time. Initially he will scratch at the collar and try to get it off. It is important that you spend time with him. Distract him with a game, chase the ball or tug-of-war – something that takes his mind off wearing the collar. Perhaps even put it on when he is about to eat his food. A soft nylon collar is least obtrusive to the puppy. Never leave a choke-chain type of collar on a puppy, as this can get him hooked up on things and nasty accidents result. Once the puppy has got used to his collar, then attach a lead to it and let him drag it around – this gets him used to the weight of the lead when it is attached. Again, do this initially just for a short time – always, of course, when you are there and can keep an eye on things.

Start by putting on the collar for short periods until the puppy gets used to it.

Photo: Kirsten Jorgensen.

Use a quiet, distraction-free area for training sessions.

When he is used to this, pick up the lead and call him to you, giving great amounts of praise and loving, so it becomes a pleasurable experience to the puppy. The blood-curdling scream and hollering that a Shiba can emit when you do something he does not accept, is like nothing you have ever heard before, and putting on a collar can be just the thing he objects the most. So, the earlier you overcome this the better. Once he accepts the confines of the collar and lead, you can walk him around the garden and then, when it is safe to take him out in public, hopefully he will walk without too much objecting!

The Shiba has a great party piece that he puts into action when you first introduce him to walking out on a lead and collar. He goes into a choking and coughing fit that is done primarily to frighten the pants off you. He then throws himself around like a demented thing, as though the collar is too tight. Finally he ends up on his back with all four legs in the air and refuses to move. *Ignore him.* He just does not like restraint or being in a controlled position. Talk to him, pet him and encourage him to walk. Let him accompany you when you

are, perhaps, walking another dog. Or get a friend to come for a walk with you with their dog. The Shiba hates to miss out on anything and it is surprising how quickly he forgets the restraints in favour of accompanied walks. This is not to say that all his misgivings about leads and collar will not return – but that is the nature of the beast! Firmness, persistence and lots of loving is the order of the day where the Shiba is concerned.

USING COMMANDS
When commanding a puppy you should use just one word, and always use the same word for the same command, otherwise it causes confusion. From birth we call all our puppies 'Puppy' when talking to them, so this becomes a familiar word to them. One of the first commands we use to the puppy is 'come', and we try making a game of it. Have someone else help you with this. Let them sit across the room from you, on the floor, of course, and have the puppy on your lap. Play with him by putting him on his back and tickling his tummy. He will usually respond by getting excited. Then have your partner call him with the words "Puppy, come" –

39

Work on the recall command from an early age, and, hopefully, your Shiba will be swift to respond.

at which point he will fly off your lap and across the floor to your partner, who then follows the same procedure for playing. Do this just a couple of times, no more, for the Shiba becomes bored very quickly. This is the beginning of training for a recall later.

For all aspects of training we use a reward, a little treat such as a small cube of cheese or chicken, plus, of course, lots of praise, "Good puppy" and a reassuring pat. If the puppy knows he is going to receive something for doing as he is asked then he will readily respond; after all, learning should be a pleasant procedure. There are many schools of thought on training; however, we have always found this one to work for us. Learning to come when he is called could save his life. Another essential command he should learn early is the Down Stay.

The Down Stay command should be initially learnt in the home and garden where the puppy is safe and secure. Having the puppy go down on all fours onto his tummy, with you by his side and the lead still attached to his collar, is the first stage. Once he has grasped this, you can detach his lead from the collar, secure in the knowledge that he will stay down and not move.

Then progress to having him go down, tell him to Stay and then walk just a pace or two out to the side of him, watching to make sure that he does not try to get up and come to you. Gradually you build up the length of time you leave him in the Down Stay position, but always be in sight of him. Give lots of praise when he completes the exercise and when you release him from the Down Stay position.

Outside your home and garden the exercise should be practised on a long training lead, which enables you to move away from your Shiba without him being unleashed. Until you are absolutely sure that you have his total attention and focus, do not chance exposing him to danger. Should he, by chance, slip his collar and lead one day when you are out walking, if he has been taught the Down Stay, you can command him and get to him before any harm might overtake him.

Always use the same command. Saying Down on one occasion and then Drop on another, only causes confusion. Try always to use just one-word commands.

40

A well-trained dog is a joy to own.

Photo: John Daniels.

Sit is a command dogs quickly learn, for it is something that comes naturally to them. Stand, for the show ring, takes a little longer. Wait is another command that dog owners use frequently; usually they command their dogs to Wait when they are putting their feed dish down for their meal. This is very necessary with large breeds but not one I use with the Shiba because of their take-it-or-leave-it attitude to food. I use Wait only when we are crossing roads.

FOCUSING ATTENTION

Training your dog to focus on you at all times is essential. The Shiba is a very alert dog, always aware of what is going on around him, and he is easily distracted. His attention span is very short, as is his concentration level. I find that constantly talking to, and involving the puppy in what I am doing, keeps his attention focused on me. Always pre-empting situations and being one step ahead of your dog is particularly important. Experienced breeders can 'read' their dogs by understanding their body language, and therefore can head off many a tricky situation before it arises – but this only comes with time and experience.

4 THE BREED STANDARDS

THE ENGLISH STANDARD

GENERAL APPEARANCE Small well balanced, sturdy dog of Spitz type. Very slightly longer than height at the withers.

CHARACTERISTICS Bright, active, keen and alert, also docile and faithful.

TEMPERAMENT Bright, active, keen and alert.

HEAD AND SKULL Head appears as a blunt triangle when viewed from above. Broad flat skull, cheeks well developed. Definite stop with slight furrow. Muzzle straight of good depth, tapering gradually. Lips tight. Black nose preferred but flesh coloured accepted in white dogs.

EYES Relatively small, almond, obliquely set well apart and dark brown.

EARS Small triangular, pricked and inclining slightly forward.

MOUTH Jaws strong with a perfect regular and complete scissors bite, i.e. upper teeth closely overlapping lower teeth and set square to the jaws.

NECK Slightly arched. Medium length, thick and muscular.

FOREQUARTERS Shoulders moderately sloping. Elbows set close to the body. Forechest well developed.Forearms straight. Pasterns slightly sloping.

BODY Withers high and well developed. Short loin, level back. Deep chest. Moderate spring of rib. Belly moderate tuck up.

HINDQUARTERS Long upper thigh, short strong second thigh. Hocks strong and parallel when seen from the rear. Turning neither in nor out. Well developed. Slight but definite bend to stifle.

FEET Cat-like, with firm, well-knuckled toes. Pads firm and elastic. Dark nails preferred.

TAIL Set on high. Thick and carried curled or curved as in a sickle.

GAIT/MOVEMENT Light, quick and energetic.

COAT Hard, straight outer coat with soft, dense undercoat. Hair on tail slightly longer.

COLOUR
Red: Intense, clear red.
Red sesame: Red with an even overlay of black guard hairs, black to be not less than 25 per cent or more than 60 per cent of normal red area.
White markings in Red and Red sesame restricted to eye spots, cheeks, underjaw, forechest, underparts and underside of tail and legs. No white above elbows or hock. The white markings on the chest resembling the shape of a bow-tie Eye spots in red sesame may be tan.
Black and tan: Dull black with a bronze cast. Tan markings restricted to eye spots, cheeks, inside of ears, legs and tail. White markings as in Red and Red sesame. Tan markings only occur between black and white areas.
White: White coat with red or grey tinges. White undercoat.

SIZE Height: Dogs 39.5cms (15.5 inches), Bitch 36.5cms (14.5 inches) with allowance of 1.5cms (.75 of an inch) either way.

FAULTS Any departure from the foregoing points should be considered a fault and the seriousness with which the fault should be regarded should be in exact proportion to its degree.

NOTE Male animals should have two apparently normal testicles fully descended into the scrotum.
Reprinted by kind permission of the Kennel Club.

THE AMERICAN KENNEL CLUB
REVISED STANDARD
MARCH 31st 1997

GENERAL APPEARANCE The Shiba is the smallest of the Japanese native breeds of dog and was originally developed for hunting by sight and scent in the dense undergrowth of Japan's mountainous areas. Alert, agile and with keen senses, he is also an excellent watchdog and companion. His frame is compact with well-developed muscles. Males and females are distinctly different in appearance: males are masculine without coarseness, females are feminine without weakness of structure.

SIZE, PROPORTION, SUBSTANCE Males 14.5 inches to 16.5 inches. Females 13.5 inches to 15.5 inches. The preferred size is the middle of the range for each sex. Average weight at preferred size is approximately 23 pounds for males and 17 pounds for females. Males have a height to length ratio of 10 to 11, females slightly longer. Bone is moderate.

HEAD Expression is good-natured with a strong and confident gaze. Eyes are somewhat triangular in shape, deep set and upward slanting toward the outside base of the ear. Iris is dark brown. Eye rim is black.

EARS Ears are triangular in shape, firmly pricked and small but in proportion to head and body size. Ears are set well apart, and tilt directly forward with a slant of the back of the ear following the arch of the neck.

HEAD Skull size is moderate and in proportion to the body. Forehead is broad and flat with a slight furrow. Stop is moderate. Muzzle is firm, full and round with a strong lower jaw projecting from full cheeks. The bridge of the muzzle is straight. Muzzle tapers slightly from the stop to nose tip. Muzzle is 40 per cent of the total head length from occiput to nose tip. It is preferred that whiskers remain intact. Lips are tight and black. Nose is black. Bite is scissors, with a full complement of strong, substantial, evenly aligned teeth. Serious Fault: Five or more missing teeth is a very serious fault and must be penalised. Disqualification: Overshot or undershot bite.

NECK, TOPLINE AND BODY The neck is thick, sturdy and of moderate length. Topline is straight and level to the base of the tail. Body is dry and well muscular without the appearance of sluggishness or coarseness. Forechest is well developed. Chest depth measured from the withers to the lowest point of the sternum is one-half or slightly less that the total height from withers to ground. Ribs are moderately sprung. Abdomen is firm and well tucked-up. Back is firm. Loins are strong. Tail is thick and powerful and is carried over the back in a sickle or curled position. A loose single curl or a sickle tail pointing vigorously toward the neck and nearly parallel to the back is preferred. A double curl or sickle tail pointing upwards is acceptable. In length the tail reaches nearly to the hock joint when extended. Tail set is high.

FOREQUARTERS Shoulder blade and upper arm are moderately angulated and approximately equal in length. Elbows are set close to the body and turn neither in nor out. Forelegs and feet are moderately spaced, straight and parallel. Pasterns are slightly inclined. Removal of front dewclaws is optional. Feet are cat-like with well arched toes fitting tightly together. Pads are thick.

HINDQUARTERS The angulation of the hindquarters is moderate and in balance with the angulation of the forequarters. Hind legs are strong with a wide natural stance. The hock joint is strong, turning neither in nor out. Upper thighs short but well developed. No dewclaws. Feet as in forequarters.

COAT Double coat, with the outer coat being stiff and straight. Fur is short and even on the face, ears and legs and should standoff the body and is about 1.5 to 2 inches in length at the withers. Tail hair is slightly longer and stands open as in a brush. It is preferred that the Shiba be presented in a natural state. Trimming of the coat must be severely penalized. Serious fault: Long or woolly coat.

COLOUR Coat colour is specified herein, with the three allowed colours given an equal consideration. All colours are clear and intense. The undercoat is cream, buff or gray. Urajiro (cream to white ventral colour) is required in the following areas on all coat colours: on the sides of the muzzle, on the cheeks, inside the ears, on the underjaw and upper throat, inside of the legs, on the abdomen, around the vent and the ventral side of the tail. On reds, commonly on the throat, forechest and the chest. On the blacks and sesames: commonly as a triangular mark on both sides of the forechest. White spots above the eyes permitted on all colours but not required.

Bright-orange red with urajiro lending a fox-like appearance to dogs of this colour. Clear red preferred but a very slight dash of black tipping is permitted on the back and tail.

Black with tan points and urajiro. Black hairs have a brownish cast, not blue. The undercoat is buff or grey. The borderline between black and tan areas is clearly defined. The Tan points are located as follows: two oval spots over the eyes; on the sides of the muzzle between the black bridge of the muzzle and the white cheeks, on the outside of the forelegs from the carpus, or a little above, downward to the toes on the outside of the hind legs down the front of the stifle broadening from hock joint to toes but not completely eliminating black from rear of pasterns. Black pencilling on toes permitted. The hairs may also be found on the inside of the ear and on the underside of the tail.

Sesame (Black tipped hairs on a rich red background) with urajiro. Tipping is light and even on the body and head with no concentration of black in any area. Sesame areas appear at least one-half red. Sesame may end in a widow's peak on the forehead, leaving the bridge and sides of the muzzle red. Eye spots and lower legs are also red.

Clearly defined white markings are permitted but not required on the tip of the tail and in the form of socks on the forelegs to the elbow joint, hind legs to the knee joint. A patch or blaze is permitted on the throat, forechest, or chest in addition to urajiro.

Serious Fault: Cream white, pinto or any other colour or markings not specified is a very serious fault and must be penalized.

GAIT Movement is nimble, light and elastic. At the trot, the legs angle in towards a centre line while the topline remains level and firm. Forward reach and rear extension are moderate and efficient. In the show ring, the Shiba is gaited on a loose lead at a brisk trot.

TEMPERAMENT A spirited boldness, a good nature and an unaffected forthrightness, which together yield dignity and natural beauty. The Shiba has an independent nature and can be reserved towards strangers but is loyal and affectionate to those who can earn his respect. At times aggressive towards other dogs, the Shiba is always under the control of his handler. Any aggression toward handler or judge or any overt shyness must be severely penalized.

SUMMARY The foregoing is a description of the ideal Shiba. Any deviation from the above Standard is to be considered a fault and must be penalized. The severity of the fault is equal to the extent of the deviation. A harmonious balance of form, colour, movement, and temperament is more critical than any one feature.

DISQUALIFICATION Males over 16.5 inches and under 14.5 inches. Females over 15.5 inches and under 13.5 inches. Overshot or undershot bite.
Reproduced by kind permission of the American Kennel Club.

FÉDÉRATION CYNOLOGIQUE INTERNATIONALE (FCI) STANDARD (Origin Japan)

UTILISATION Hunting dog for birds and small animals. Companion dog.

FCI'S CLASSIFICATION Group: 5 (Spitz and primitive types) Section 5 (Asian Spitz and related breeds). Without working trials.

BRIEF HISTORICAL SUMMARY The Shiba has been a native breed to Japan since the primitive ages. The word 'Shiba' originally refers to something 'small', a 'small dog'. The Shiba's habitat was in the mountainous area facing the Sea of Japan and the Shiba was used as a hunting dog for small animals and birds. There were slight differences in the breeds according to the area where they were raised. As dogs like English Setters and English Pointers were imported from England during the period of 1868-1912, hunting became a sport in Japan and cross breeding of the Shiba with those English dogs became prevalent and a pure Shiba became rare so that by 1912-1926 pure Shibas confined to these areas became exceedingly scarce. Hunters and other educated persons became concerned with the preservation of the pure Shibas from around 1928 and the preservation of the limited number of pure strains began seriously, and the breed standards were finally unified in 1934. In 1937 the Shiba was designated as a Natural Monument after which the breed was bred and improved to become the superior breed known today.

GENERAL APPEARANCE Small-sized dog, well balanced, well-boned with well developed muscles. Constitution strong. Action quick, free and beautiful.

IMPORTANT PROPORTIONS The ratio of height at withers to length of body is 10-11.

BEHAVIOUR AND TEMPERAMENT The temperament is faithful, with keenness in sense and high alertness.

HEAD Forehead broad, cheeks well developed and stop defined with slight furrow. Nasal bridge straight and nose black in colour desirable. Muzzle moderately thick and tapering. Lips tight and teeth strong with scissor bite.

EYES Relatively small, triangular and dark brown in colour, the corners of the eyes are upturned.

EARS Relatively small, triangular, slightly inclining forward and firmly pricked.

NECK Thick, strong, and well balanced with the head and the body.

BODY Back straight and strong, loin broad and muscular. Chest deep, ribs moderately sprung, belly well drawn up.

TAIL Set on high, thick, carried vigorously curled or curved as a sickle, the tip nearly reaching hocks when let down.

FOREQUARTERS Shoulders moderately sloping, elbows tight, seen from the front, forelegs straight.

HINDQUARTERS Upper thighs long, lower thighs short, but well developed. Hocks thick and tough.

FEET Digits tightly closed and well arched. Pads hard and elastic. Nails hard and dark in colour desirable.

GAIT Light and brisk.

COAT HAIR Outer coat harsh and straight, undercoat soft and dense, hair on tail slightly long and standing off.

COLOUR Red, black and tan, sesame, black sesame, red sesame. Definition of the colour sesame:
Sesame: Equal mixture of white and black hairs.
Black sesame: More black than white hairs.
Red sesame: Ground colour of hair red, mixture with black hairs.

All of the above colours must have "Urajiro".
"Urajiro": Whitish coat on the sides of the muzzle and on the cheeks, on the underside of the jaw and neck, on the chest and stomach and the underside of the tail, and on the inside of the legs.

SIZE Height at withers: Dogs 40cm (15.75 inches) bitches 37cm (14.6 inches). There is a tolerance of 1.5cm smaller or taller. Dogs 15.1 inches to 16.3 inches and bitches 14 inches to 15.2 inches.

FAULTS Any departure from the foregoing points should be considered as a fault and the seriousness with which the fault should be regarded should be in exact proportion to its degree.
1)   Shyness
2)   Bitchy dogs, doggy bitches.
3)   Malocclusion (Overshot or Undershot mouth).
4)   Numerous teeth missing.

DISQUALIFYING FAULTS
1) **Ears not pricked.**
2) **Hanging or short tail.**

NB Male animals should have two apparently normal testicles fully descended into the scrotum.

DISCUSSION OF THE STANDARDS

DISTINCTION BETWEEN MALES AND FEMALES

A distinct difference between the male and the female of the breed is essential. Of course, at a glance the sexual organs will tell us which is the male and which is the female. Masculinity in the male should be very apparent, as should the femininity in the female. The male overall should exude his masculine aura.

The distinction between males and females is said to be an important characteristic of higher animals. It has been noted that the more highly developed a species is, in the animal world, the more pronounced are the sex differences. The Japanese thus require their dogs to be distinct in sexual differences, thus reflecting the view that the dog is one of the most highly developed of animals.

The body stature and size should immediately differentiate the male from the female. The male should be taller and more muscular, with a ratio of 10 to 11; the female should be slightly longer. The height of the male should be 39.5cm and that of the female should be 36.5cm. A range tolerance of 1.5cm taller or shorter is allowed.

The way the male stands, the way he moves and the way he promotes himself, should convey confidence at all times,

with no sign of timidity. He should always appear to be in control of himself and his surroundings. The male's features should reflect a masculine nobility and dignity. His head, skull and facial bones are wider and longer than those of the female. The forehead is wide and flat with full pouch-like cheeks. He should have a thick strong muzzle, his eyes should reflect a steady gaze of confidence and strength, while the female's head is slightly narrower and finer in construction, with a softness in the expression.

In overall construction the male should be stockier and heavier in bone than the female. His muscles should be well-defined and he should exude a robust and vigorous appearance. The female should be lighter in bone, and more refined in appearance, with an air of femininity and softness. These sexual differences in the male and the female are essential; and all the more so when breeding for the preservation and correctness of type and improvements for the future breeding programmes.

TYPE AND BALANCE

All domestic animals are bred for a certain 'type'. This distinguishes one breed from another. It is by breeding, showing and judging that one hopes to improve one's stock to achieve the Standard for the breed. Each breed has a Standard to work to. By reading and understanding the Japanese Standard for the dog, we begin to understand the harmony of build and construction necessary.

Balance (equilibrium) and harmony of build are mentioned in the Standard. Balance is linked with structure of the

The Shiba Inu must display harmony and symmetry in its make-up.

dog and the two go hand-in-hand towards purpose and function which is essential to any breed. Balance is 'harmony and symmetry in the dog's make-up that comes from an alliance of each body part being in unison, i.e. the head, neck, trunk and all four legs.'

Equilibrium means that both sides of the scale are equal. Thus any imbalance in the dog will show and be detrimental to him, e.g. if the head and shoulders of the dog are well developed and the rear end tails off or lacks substance, then the dog is unbalanced. Because of his imbalance he will not move correctly and, standing, he will look unbalanced.

Harmony means that all parts of the dog are in unison, e.g. a long body is not in harmony with short legs visually, and the dog will move in a cramped style.

BODY PROPORTIONS
The Japanese Standard is about body proportions or balance as we term it. They use something called the "parallel quadrangle" to illustrate this. If we think of the Shiba as 100 or 100 per cent, the Japanese apportion tables thus:-
If the body height is 100 then the body length is 110
If the body height is 100 then chest depth is 45 per cent and the legs 55 per

BODY PROPORTIONS
Line drawings: Viv Rainsbury.

CORRECT
PROPORTIONS OF
THE SHIBA INU

A. Fore-body
B. Mid-body
C. Rear-body
D. Chest depth
E. Elbow to ground
E. + D. Height
F. Body length
G. Muzzle length
H. Backskull length
G. + H. Head length
I. Face width
J. Chest width
K. Pastern circumference
L. Hip width

RATIOS

If height = 100:
Length = 110
Pastern Circumf. = 19 – 20
Hip width = 18 – 20
Chest depth = 45 – 50
Chest circumf. = 116 – 120
Chest width = 36 – 38

If Length = 100:
Fore = 28.5
Mid = 43
Rear = 28.5

If Head length = 100:
Muzzle length = 40
Face width = 56 – 58.

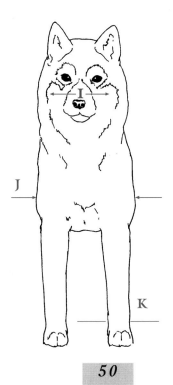

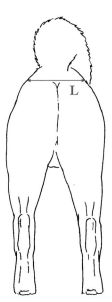

cent. Knowing the height, length and head length of the Shiba then gives us a basis to work on for all the other measurements and angles. The weight of an average Shiba should be 10kg (22lbs), the male being 10 per cent more than this and the female being 10 per cent less.

The Shiba body and its angles are all important. Angles of the body in respect of the balance of the Shiba have to be considered. The overall appearance of the Shiba should be one of just 'off-square'. When he is mature his chest should be wide and deep, reaching to his elbows. His legs should be of good length and correct proportions to his body, not short and giving the appearance of being stocky and unbalanced; neither should the legs be too long and stilt-like, thus throwing out the balance of the Shiba. The correct proportions and angulation of the legs to the body is important in giving the dog the greatest amount of mobility and drive with maximum efficiency in his gait.

By illustrating in diagrams the angles and proportions of the Shiba it is easier to understand what comprises the whole dog. As with all breeds the head-piece is the breed. Looking at the Shiba's head it is a symphony of triangles (or blunt wedges). The ears are wedge-shaped and the head as a whole is wedge-shaped

The head has a prominent bump called the occiput. It can be felt between the ears and defines the end of the skull, and from this point can be measured the length of the skull and total head length. The total length of the head is made up of the muzzle and the back skull length combined. The back-skull makes up 60 per cent and the muzzle makes up the other 40 per cent of the total head length. The middle of the stop can be accurately pin-pointed by drawing an imaginary line from the inner corners of the eyes and placing it in the centre. The width of the head is determined by the spread of the cheekbones.

THE NECK
The neck of the Shiba should be well developed, thick and sturdy. The skin of the neck should appear closely attached; when it appears loose or slack it gives the impression of an old dog or an out-of-condition dog. The male's neck should appear brawny while the female's neck should appear refined. The neck of the Shiba gives the impression of being shorter than that of the medium-size breeds of Japanese dogs. It is difficult to give a neck ratio for the Shiba as the thickness of the neck has to be included in the equation, and this can vary from dog to dog, but again the balance and harmony in relation to the overall dog is what defines correct and incorrect neck length. When on the move at a trot the head is carried lower than when the Shiba is standing; but when the Shiba is sprinting fast, the neck extends almost parallel to the ground, thus moving the centre of gravity forward, allowing the rear legs to move more freely and propel the body faster.

THE MUZZLE
The muzzle of the Shiba should be firm, and taper from where it begins at the stop to the end of the nose, thus giving it a wedge shape in appearance. The tapering should be gradual. The sides of the muzzle should be 'thick, full and round' giving the impression of strength.

HEAD AND MUZZLE

The head in profile.
1. The forehead is broad and flat.
2. The cheeks are full.
3. The stop is moderate.
4. The bridge of the nose is straight.
5. The upper and lower lips
are black and light.

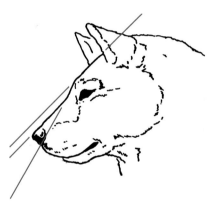

The face is too flat. The line of the forehead and muzzle are too close together.

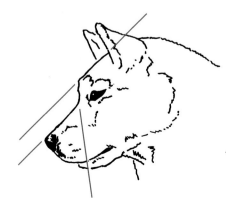

The stop is too steep. The lines of the forehead and muzzle are too far apart.

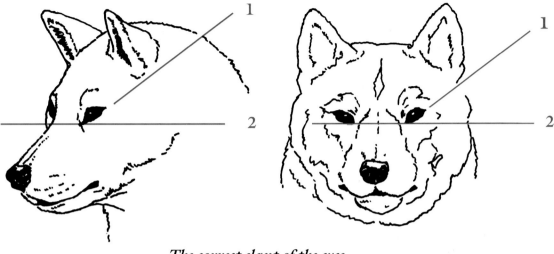

The correct slant of the eyes.
1. A straight line connects the inner corners of the eyes.

2. A line is drawn from the inner corner of the eye through to the outer corner of the ear.

The width and depth of the muzzle, and the appearance of strength it gives, will vary somewhat in the male and the female, remembering the male's masculinity and the female's femininity. There should be no dew-lap. The lips should be tight and the pigment of the lips should be black, as should the nose. The nose should be hard and, in a healthy dog, the nose should be cold and moist.

THE CHEEKS

The Shiba has very full cheeks, giving a wider appearance to the head than in most other breeds. The forehead should be broad and flat. In profile, or full face, there should be no bump or bulge apparent. While there is a slight shallow groove from the centre of the fore-head down to the stop, it should be hardly visible. There should be no wrinkle or deep groove. The full pouch-like cheeks in the Shiba are his trade mark; they are his special characteristic along with his hooded ears and spirited boldness of temperament that sets him apart from the rest.

The tight tapering muzzle only goes to emphasise the full cheeks, and this contrast subsequently highlights his facial and expressional characteristics. The stop marks the point where the head changes from the broad forehead and pouched cheeks to the tapering muzzle. The stop should be a gentle, moderate stop. A steep stop or a flat stop are both equally undesirable.

THE EYES

The eyes should be very dark brown (but they should not be black) and slightly tipping up at the outside corners. The slant of the outside corner of the eye should continue on an imaginary line to touch the side of the head just about at base of the ear lobe. Small eyes are preferred for the Shiba, though in the female, with her finer head, her eyes may appear larger than those of the male. The eyes, as with the ears, must blend in with the rest of the head. The set of the eyes is important to the overall expression and composition of the head. Eyes sitting too shallow in the sockets give a 'bulging' eye appearance. Eyes too close together give a harsh, flighty appearance, and eyes set wide apart seem to make the features 'open up'. Because of the smallness of the Shiba, and the size of their eyes in relation to the size of their heads, sometimes it means that they are prone to having large, round eyes, which is a definite fault. Their eyes should reflect their innermost thoughts. The dog's eye expressions are the human's main way of understanding what the dog is feeling, and they are Shiba's way of transmitting his feelings to the human. The Shiba's eye should convey, with a steady, constant gaze, confidence and composure, his loyalty to you and a spirited boldness and intelligence. A shifty, restless gaze only conveys uneasiness, suspicion and uncertainty.

THE EARS
The ears of the Shiba, and the aesthetic appearance they give to the head of the Shiba, is paramount. The ear placement, shape and size have to be in harmony and balance with the total head. The ears should be small and triangular-shaped, tipping slightly forward and set firm on the head. Ears that are too large give a coarse appearance to the head. The triangular shape should be the isosceles triangle, with the two equal sides being

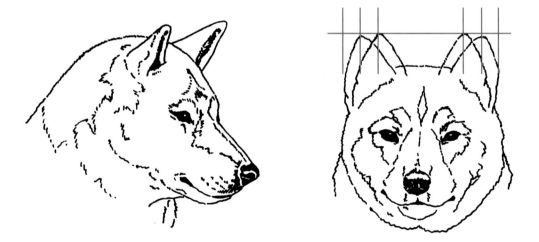

LEFT: Correct ears showing hooded effect.
RIGHT. Correct ears showing the triangular ear shape and correct placement on the head. The outer ear sides extend down the outer sides of the head providing the limits within the width of the head that the ears should sit.

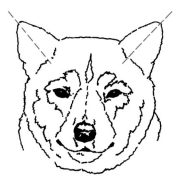

Incorrect: The ears slant towards each other.

Incorrect: The ears slant out to the side of the head.

Incorrect: The dog-leg curve at the base of the outer line spoils the triangular appearance.

the sides of the ears; this balanced appearance should be seen when looking full face on at the Shiba, though in fact the sides of the ears on the Shiba are extended slightly down on either side of the head. The inner line appears shorter and arched, while the base of the ear is broad and the set is reasonably far apart with forward slant. Correct ear placement on the head is vital. Ears set too high on the head or too low on the side of the head are incorrect, as are ears that are set too close together or too far apart.

The inclination forward of the ear should give a hooded effect. The firm set and erectness of the ears relies on the ears being of correct thickness and texture. When on the move the ears should remain upright and firm; there should be no swaying or flapping. The mental state of the Shiba can be reflected in his ear carriage. A relaxed dog may carry his ears out to the side, while a nervous dog will flatten his ears in a submissive way. The correct ear carriage in the Shiba reflects his calmness and his confidence in his own ability.

TEETH

The teeth of the Shiba, as in all breeds, are important, for, once breeders start to relax their views and requirements in relation to full dentition in a breed, the mouth of that breed suffers in the long term. The fact that the domesticated dog does not have to forage, seek out and kill its next meal, as it would in the wild, using his mouth and teeth for the kill and the eventual devouring of his prey, is no excuse for allowing his mouth to deviate from the requirement of a full complement of teeth to do the job. The Shiba's teeth are his only means of defence.

Puppies begin to develop their milk teeth at three to four weeks of age. The milk teeth consist of twelve incisors, four

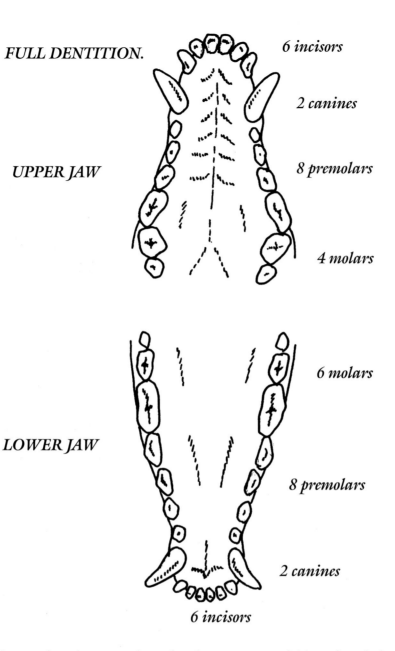

FULL DENTITION.

6 incisors

2 canines

UPPER JAW

8 premolars

4 molars

6 molars

LOWER JAW

8 premolars

2 canines

6 incisors

canines and twelve premolars; they have usually appeared by the time the puppy is eight to ten weeks old.

The Shiba seems particularly prone to missing teeth. The first premolars are usually the teeth that are missing in the Shiba (and many other breeds too). When considering the size of the Shiba's head and mouth and the size of his adult teeth, six incisors top and bottom seem

an awful lot of teeth for such a small mouth, and sometimes these appear crowded in the mouth.

A full complement of teeth in the Shiba is forty-two teeth, and while he may well be able to manage quite happily with forty-one or even forty, it is a slippery slide that you are embarking on and one hard to reverse, once set on that path. Full dentition requires the

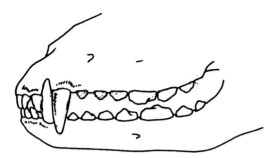

Scissor bite: The top incisors just overlap the bottom.

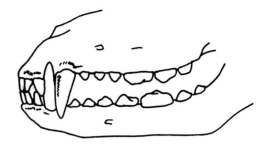

Even bite: Incisors meet level or even.

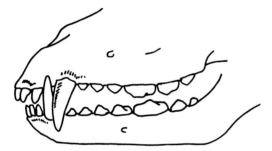

Overshot: A gap between the incisors due to the face being too long or the jaw being too short.

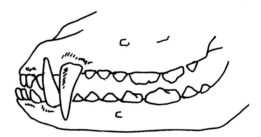

Undershot bite: There is a gap between the incisors due to the face being too short or the jaw being too long.

Shiba to have six incisors, two canines, eight premolars and four molars in the upper jaw and six molars, eight premolars, two canines and six incisors in the bottom jaw.

BITE

While the face and the jaw growth will determine the type of bite your Shiba will have inherited, he will be required to have a scissor bite with the canines and incisors fitting close together when the mouth is closed. The top incisors should overlap the bottom teeth with the backs of the top teeth touching the fronts of the bottom teeth. The rest of the teeth then interlock with each other. If there is a gap between the top and the bottom teeth then the mouth is overshot or undershot. If the incisors meet tip to tip then this is a level bite. Though this is considered acceptable, it can make it difficult for the Shiba to close its mouth properly, and can cause wear and tear on the teeth as time passes. Each side of the face and jaw grows independently of the other and, though the incisors may fit closely together, sometimes it may be undershot on one side and overshot on the other side; this is called a wry mouth.

Retained teeth can cause maximum problems in the mouth of the Shiba. It is important when your Shiba is teething that you keep a very close eye on the mouth, for what sometimes happens is that the milk teeth do not loosen and drop out, and the adult tooth can continue to grow either alongside or behind the milk tooth that has been retained, thus causing a distortion of the correct line for the teeth. The adult teeth, having grown out of alignment (even after the milk teeth have been removed or have fallen out) are now not in a true position and this can cause a bad bite eventually when all the adult teeth have appeared. If you observe this happening it is important to have the milk tooth removed as soon as you are aware of the adult tooth's predicament. It must have a clear place in which to grow through. The occasional incisor may be missing in the puppy's mouth, but this does not automatically mean that the adult top incisors will be missing. At eight weeks and over, the two fang-like teeth (canines) should have appeared on either side of the incisors, both top and bottom; these should interlock with each other so that the bottom fang nestles between the top fang and the last incisor when the mouth is closed.

On each side of the top jaw and each side of the bottom jaw, directly behind the canines, are the premolars, four on each side. The premolars increase in size as they go to the back of the mouth. In the puppy mouth there are three premolars on either side top and bottom. There should be a gap between the puppy canines and the premolars.

Complete dentition in the puppy prior to the eruption of his baby teeth at around four months should be twenty-eight baby teeth. The molars are the final group of teeth. In the adult mouth there should be two on each side in the upper jaw and three on each side of the bottom jaw. The first of these molars is large, the remaining two behind are somewhat smaller and not easy to see. The last molar may not appear until eight to ten months of age. Because of its smallness it is sometimes missed by breeders, judges and vets when examining the mouth.

THE BODY AND LEGS

The front and back legs of the Shiba must work together to move the body correctly. It is important that they are in harmony together. Angulation in the front legs must be pertinent for the rear legs. Over-angulation in both the front and rear legs, while not allowing the dog to move very well, would be better than a dog over-angulated in the rear and straight in front. Legs should have correct muscle development and be of correct length in relation to each other, for too long legs in the front will only serve to throw off balance the dog in movement and when standing, as would short front legs and long rear legs. The Shiba must, in repose, stand four-square and sound.

Shoulders should be moderately angulated. A '45 degree layback' was until recently considered the ideal. But much research has now in fact revealed that a 30 degree layback angle is more conducive to dogs moving properly.

The foreleg bone and the upper arm are connected by the elbow joint; thus the upper arm bone should fit tightly to

Correct front

*Incorrect:
Pigeon-toed.*

*Incorrect:
Too narrow.*

*Incorrect:
Too wide.*

*Incorrect:
'9 o'clock-3 o'clock'.*

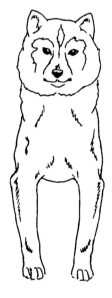

*Incorrect:
Bowed-out at elbows.*

*Incorrect:
Chippendale.*

A

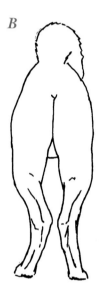

D

REARS

A. *Correct rear.*

B. *Incorrect: Cow-hocked.*

C. *Incorrect: Too wide.*

D. *Incorrect: Too narrow.*

E. *Weak, over-angulated.*

B

C

E

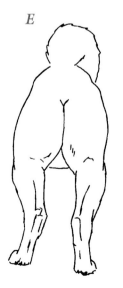

the trunk of the Shiba. If it does not, then the elbows will bow out; conversely, if the upper arm bone is too close it appears squeezed and narrow.

The pasterns should be moderate in length and have a slight forward slant. They should not point in nor out. The feet should have high arched toes giving a moderate thickness to the feet. Gaps between the toes are unsightly and resemble a hare foot. A tight, cat-like foot is the ideal. Toe-nails should be black, short and hard. If the feet are correct the nails will be in contact with the ground and, with moderate wear and tear, they will remain short and hard.

The rear legs are the driving power for the Shiba and it is the rear legs that set movement in motion. The rear legs must be strong and flexible. While the forelegs bear the bulk of the Shiba, it is the rear legs that propel the Shiba forward. Viewed from the rear, the legs are parallel and the width of the stance matches the width of the hips. Too 'narrow' a stance, and too 'wide' a stance, and the 'bowed-out' stance, are all considered faults. Rear angulation should be moderate in the stifle of the Shiba; over-angulation or straight stifles are incorrect, and will affect the way the Shiba gaits.

The Japanese standard requires the chest to be deep and the ribs moderately sprung with a well-developed fore-chest. The chest appears to be the centre of the whole of the body, and is the overall influence in respect of the outline of the body and the contrasts with the tuck-up of the stomach. A powerful chest denotes a feeling of strength in the dog. Chest width is assessed by measuring the area between the left and the right shoulder joints. The shoulder joints are the joints between the shoulder blade and the upper fore leg bones and this is the widest part of the chest. The structure and width of the forechest are important in deciding if the dog will have correct structure and movement in his forelegs.

The bones and tendons and muscles in the forechest must be well developed. Viewed from the front the shoulder joints should not protrude. If the forechest is not correct it will affect the gait of the dog; he will not be sound and the reach of the forelegs will be hampered. His natural pose, when standing, will also be affected. The chest depth is determined by measuring from the highest point of the withers to the bottom of the chest at the point of the elbows. Chest depth should be almost half the body height. Between 45 per cent and 50 per cent is good. Chest width should be measured at the widest part of the outward curve (the breast or chest wall should be shaped like an upside-down egg). As the heart and lungs are housed within, it is important that the cavity is large enough to accommodate them. Flat-chests or barrel-chests are very detrimental to the dog. Having the correct egg-shaped breast allows the Shiba, when running and using up a great deal of energy, to move large quantities of air into and out of his lungs, and his ribs need to be flexible enough to accommodate this. The most flexible ribs are the long ribs which provide sufficient room in the breast cavity, and allow the lungs to function correctly, when put under stress. Barrel-shaped ribs, though providing space in the breast cavity, are not capable of contracting as well as the longer ribs

in the egg shape, and thus air is not able to pump so freely through, when needed. Likewise, flat ribs constrict the space occupied by the heart and the lungs and they, in turn, are incapable of good expansion and contraction.

The top-line should be level from the neck to the base of the tail, enabling the Shiba to move straight, firm and all together. A roached back, apart from looking unsightly, affects the entire topline, and so affects the movement of the dog. A saggy back, though more common, also badly affects the movement and the topline in the Shiba and, when viewed from the rear, on the move, the dog appears to sway from side to side in a 'fish-tail'-like movement. If the back is too long, or the Shiba has been overfed and under-exercised, a saggy back will be the result.

THE TAIL
The tail of the Shiba is his crowning glory and, like his hooded ears, is what makes him stand out from all other breeds of dog. It should be thick, and powerful. This means that the tail vertebrae (the bones that make up the tail) should be thick. Though the hair on the tail is thick and plush, it is also slightly longer than that on the rest of the Shiba's body. A thin, weak tail does nothing to convey the strength and power that the Japanese require to be apparent in their Shibas.

The tail can be either sickle or curled and, when extended, should reach to his hocks. It can curl either over his right or his left side, though curling to the left seems the more common. There are four commonly seen shapes of the curled tail. The tail should be powerful in a way that

Correct: The single curl is the most desirable. It appears relaxed, and beautifully inclined and flexible when on the move, giving the Shiba balance and mobility. It conveys a calm, confident temperament.

The double curl is a tight curl. It does not convey the same composure and beauty as the single curl, nor does it give the Shiba the same fluid mobility

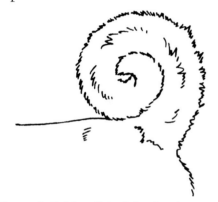

The curl of this tail is tight, but its actual position on the back of the dog is high and it looks like an afterthought.

A slack tail: This looks weak and does not convey good temperamental qualities.

Sickle tail: This is permissible in the Shiba because of his body type and the quickness and lightness needed by him in the type of hunting he would pursue in the wilds. The sickle tail expresses vigour and quickness, while aiding movement.

expresses the vigour and strength of the dog. It should denote how quick and agile the Shiba is. The tail is also the rudder of the dog; it helps him make quick, efficient changes in direction as and when necessary, when pursuing quarry when out hunting.

GAIT
Gait in the Shiba is judged mainly at the trot. The diagonal legs always move together, with the driving power in the rear legs. The dog's body moves forward by reaching with his rear legs and grabbing the ground firmly; his front legs move forward with the shift of his body weight. While the diagonal legs move together, the front legs move forward fractionally earlier than the rear legs. When observing from the side the well-constructed dog's gait, we see that the rear legs land at the same point at which the front legs landed. The rear legs kick the ground powerfully while the front legs move forward smoothly, creating the quick action and nimble

elastic steps mentioned in the Standard. The legs should land close to the centre line of the body's gravity in order to maintain equilibrium in motion. They do not, however, totally single-track, but move leaving steps that almost meet at the centre line. Observing the Shiba's gait while he is trotting naturally should be done from the side as well as from the back. It is important that the Shiba is gaited by his handler at the correct speed for him. Knowing the correct pace for your Shiba comes only with practice. The dog with a good gait has good bone construction, firm tendons, a solid body and a good nature.

COAT COLOUR
Coat colour of the Shiba Inu, and the white markings called 'ghosting', are very important.
RED The outer coat should be deep rich clear red. The undercoat should be a blue/grey.
BLACK, TAN AND WHITE The outer coat should be a dull black with a rusty

Red: This should be a deep, rich colour

Photo: John Daniels.

LEFT: Black, tan and white, with bow-tie markings.
Photo: John Daniels.

ABOVE:. White: The outer coat can have red or grey tinges.

Red sesame: The outer coat is a mixture of red and black hairs.

Photo: Marilyn Packer.

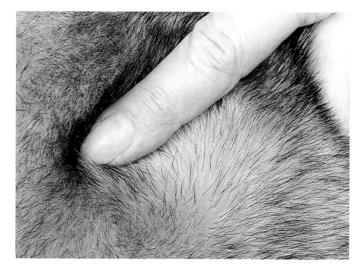

A close-up of the colours in a sesame coat.

Photo: John Daniels.

hue. The coat should not be a shiny jet black. The undercoat should be red/fawn. Tan markings should be between the black and white on the face, and on the legs and with the small tan spots above the eyes.

RED SESAME (Aka Goma) The outer coat should have an even all-over mixture of red and black hairs; there should not be less there 50 per cent red. The undercoat should be red/fawn.

WHITE The outer coat white with red or grey tinges. The undercoat white.

GHOSTING OR URIJIRO This should be on the following areas only:-

1) The sides of the muzzle and the cheeks, not to extend over the bridge of the nose. Small white spots above the eyes on red and red sesame.

2) On each underneath section of the jaw, neck, chest and stomach. On the forechest extending as far as the shoulder joint but not extending onto the shoulder.

3) White is permissible on the legs but must not go past the elbows on the forelegs or knee joint on back legs.

4) A white tip to the tail is permissible.

The outer coat is harsh and straight.

Photo: Lyn Lane.

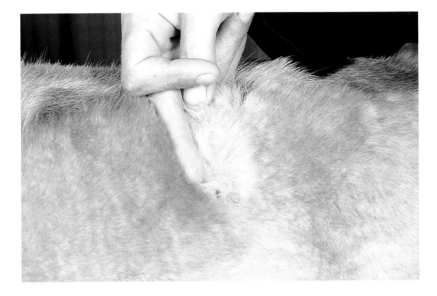

The undercoat is soft and dense.

Photo: John Daniels.

White markings, other than those described, on any other part of the body are very undesirable. A complete white face, known as a reverse mask, is also undesirable. White on the forechest of a black, white and tan gives the appearance of a bow tie. Brindle is not a colour seen in the Shiba in Japan.

In the sesame more than 50 per cent of black hairs on red is a black sesame and this is undesirable. Too much tan on the head, neck, back or trunk of the black, white and tan Shiba is also undesirable. There should also not be any spots or flecking on the white markings. White Shibas are not shown in Japan. Colour fades in the aged Shiba, and while the Shiba is going through a moult.

COAT
The guard (surface) hairs must be needle thick, strong and straight. The undercoat must be soft and dense.

5 *THE SHOW RING*

All aspects of training have to be started early with your Shiba. Whether you want to show, or just to have a happy sociable dog, this rule applies. The Shiba enjoys company and this enjoyment needs to be encouraged and maintained. The Shiba is only as good as the person that moulds his character. If you treat him as a wild animal, that is how he will behave. Keep him kennelled and short of companionship and he will go his own way and revert back to nature, where he is suspicious and wary of all that he comes into contact with.

GAINING YOUR SHIBA'S CONFIDENCE

Socialising is the key factor in his training and this applies to humans as well as other animals. He will readily love adults and children but will not

Crufts 1992 – the first Shiba classes scheduled at the UK's most prestigious show. Liz Dunhill (left) is pictured with Wellshim Black Jack is Vormund (Best of Breed and Best Dog), and the author is with Madason Toya (Best Bitch).

Photo: David Dalton.

tolerate rough handling or abuse. Firm and fair are the rules to success. By nature the Shiba is independent. Self-preservation comes naturally to him, and left to his own devices boredom will set in and mischief will quickly follow. He is not by nature a social or a civilised being and he will battle most of the time against turning into one, so you must be firm and persistent in your efforts to persuade him that this is the way it is and that this is the way it will be.

Whatever you do, in your pursuit of making your Shiba happy, you must always do it with love, for, like people, these dogs respond best to love. Kindness and affection conquer mountains. When reprimanding your puppy or your adult dog for a misdemeanour, remember to follow it up with a show of affection, so that he realises that you are only trying to explain what you wish of him. He needs to know that you still love him and that the punishment was for doing something not acceptable, albeit for something he did not know was wrong. Shibas are quick to learn and will learn from you as the alpha being. It is important to show affection in all the things you do with your puppy, whether it is feeding or training or even when you have to give him medication. All experiences for the Shiba initially should be pleasant experiences. Affection is catching! If you love him he will respond accordingly. If you show him respect he will, equally, respond with respect. This is the time to gain your puppy's confidence and respect which, as his teacher, you must do, for now as well as the future.

As I have said before, the Shiba is not a dog for the faint-hearted. Once you have gained his trust and loyalty, the rewards are great, for you will not find a more loving, more pleasurable or greater companion than the Shiba. His love just oozes from those almond eyes, and his constant attention makes it all worthwhile.

THE SHIBA IN THE SHOW RING

The Japanese Shiba Inu in the show-ring is a riveting sight. His bright, pristine colours, glorious fur coat, and his alert, confident and composed stance, together with his quick and nimble movements, make him stand out from the rest of the breeds – a striking show dog, without a doubt. To exhibit pedigree dogs is a great pleasure and hobby. It is fun and it is sociable for both exhibitor and exhibit – the dogs can and do enjoy it as much as their owners do. Some dogs have a natural affinity with the show ring, and the minute they walk into the ring they seem to come alive; like actors on a stage, they take on a whole new meaning.

The real purpose of showing at dog shows is to compare the apple of your eye with the other dogs in your breed and to get the unbiased opinion of the judge. Of course different people see different things, but as time goes by you will get a fairly good idea of what is required. If you have bought a good specimen of the breed you will want to be sure that other breeders and judges confirm this. Winning is not the be all and end all. But you do need to know that, from a breeding point of view, your dog or bitch would be suitable, for only the best stock should be selected to breed from to produce the next generations.

At six weeks, this puppy is learning to stand on the table.

Photo: John Daniels.

The Shiba soon learns to be relaxed when he is being handled.

HANDLING THE SHIBA

Show training should have begun at about five to six weeks of age, once the puppy is up on his feet and steady. If you are going to show your puppy, you never tell him to 'sit', for in the show ring he must 'stand' at all times for the judge to go over him. When you are playing with him, gently stand him four square, supporting him and encouraging him in a calm manner and in a reassuring way, so that he becomes used to being handled by you in a positive fashion. When he accepts this routine, which usually takes a couple of weeks, you then progress to standing him on a table top.

POSING THE SHIBA INU

ABOVE: The Shiba's natural stance shows its conformation off to full advantage. The dog must be trained to pose like this in the show ring.

Photo: Lyn Lane.

BELOW: Show stance demonstrated by Madason Mister Ry, aged ten months.

A grooming table with a non-slip top is ideal. This will also be where he will be groomed, and early exposure to this is also essential and should become the norm.

Be very careful and reassuring when you first lift the puppy up onto the table top. Gently place him down, firmly supporting him so that he has no fear of the height or of falling. If you can get one of the family or a friend to gently go over him while he is standing, so much the better. Sometimes the puppy will turn round quickly if he is being handled on his rear end, so reassure him and pet him while this is happening, so that he readily accepts the procedure. He will need to be used to other people looking in his mouth and, again, this should be done from a very early age, firstly by you examining his teeth and then by other family members doing the same – but always this should be done with care and respect for him, and with no rough handling, and with you talking to him all the time.

THE SHIBA SHAKE
Moving correctly on the lead is the next important phase. He will already be used to walking on the lead. You need also now to train him in the correct movement and pace for the show ring and on how to come to a halt before the judge and stand in a confident stance, looking attentive. This might be the right time to mention the 'The Shiba Shake'. This usually takes place when you have the dog in a controlled situation, having taken him down from the examination table and placed him on the floor to move him out from the judge. He will go into a complete body shake from head to tail, all at once. Trying to correct him while this is going on is a waste of time. Just be patient, let him finish, then continue to move him out. If you persist in pulling him to move while he is performing the 'shake' he will only

stop and do it again, such is his determination. There is no logical explanation for his action, but it would seem feasible that, having been restrained on the table, he feels the need to "shake" free and be in control of his person.

LEARNING FROM SHOWS
Attending shows and watching how the professionals handle their dogs is the best way for you to learn. Speaking to them and asking for their help and advice, and also asking if they have any tips they can give you in the early days, can all be beneficial to you. But do be careful not to intrude on them if they are preparing to go into the ring, or at a time that is bad for them. However, given that you choose the right moment, never be scared to ask for advice. It is the only way to learn.

Lots of love and encouragement are the secret in the early days. You build up your very close bond with your Shiba by spending time together daily, and gaining each other's confidence and affection. Persuading him that showing is fun, and that it can be rewarding, will make it something he can look forward to.

TRAINING CLASSES
Attending a local training class should begin as soon as the puppy is safe to mix with other dogs – this is when all his injections have been administered and the vet gives you the OK to take him out and about in public. Usually there are classes for the absolute beginner, and this is where you start. Having found out when the classes are held, go along with your dog and for the first couple of visits just sit with your Shiba and observe. This gives your dog time to get used to other people and dogs in a close environment before he begins his training in earnest. Most training clubs have general dog training classes and also show and beauty classes, and you will need to talk through with the trainer what you wish to pursue. What you learn at the classes needs to be put in to practice at home on a daily basis.

HELP FROM THE BREEDER
Keeping in touch with the breeder from whom you purchased your puppy is important. Most breeders are only too pleased to help and encourage their puppies' new owners. If you are aspiring to show the puppy, it is important to let the breeders see him from time to time and get their opinion as to how they think the puppy is progressing and whether or not they think he is up to being shown. Some puppies take longer to mature than others. Never be in too much of a hurry to get him into the ring. Better to wait till he is just right for showing. It is amazing what long memories some folk have. Some shortcoming in a puppy in his early showing days can follow him for the rest of his show life – or so it would seem.

MATCH EVENINGS
Most training classes hold match evenings where you have the opportunity of competing against other dogs in the club. This is an excellent way to introduce your puppy to the show world in a sociable and friendly environment. It gets the puppy used to being handled and moved, and used to the atmosphere that prevails at shows. It also helps you, the owner, by giving you the chance to assess your dog's attitude to showing.

STACKING THE SHIBA INU
Photos: John Daniels.

TOP LEFT: Step One: The Shiba can be manoeuvred into the correct show stance. This is known as stacking.

TOP RIGHT: Step Two: The hindlegs are placed.

LEFT: Step Three: The lead is held taut, encouraging the Shiba to maintain the pose.

Does he quickly get bored? If so, stand at the beginning of the line for your assessment when showing. Or does he need time to settle once you go in the ring? If so, then stand down the line before your assessment. What is his concentration span? Does he need something to focus on? Remember, whatever you choose to use to keep your dog's concentration on you, it should not interfere with anyone else in the show ring. Many exhibitors use squeaky toys or throw baiting treats that distract other people's dogs. This is extremely bad manners and fools nobody! It is just not done in the big ring among the professionals.

OPEN SHOWS

The next stage to showing your puppy should be entering in the Open shows or smaller local shows; this is all excellent grounding for novice people and dogs, and many well-seasoned campaigners introduce the new shining lights to the show scene this way. It gives you a good idea about how your puppy compares with others around and what, if anything, you can do to improve him.

It will also give you the opportunity of meeting breeders and exhibitors. There may be questions you need to get answers to, or information you require, and again it is a super way to introduce yourself and your dog to others that are already part of your chosen breed. For sure there is always something that you can learn, no matter how long you have owned and been around dogs.

ENTERING SHOWS

To help you keep abreast of the dog scene there are numerous publications available, either weekly or monthly. In the weekly publications you have correspondents who write on their particular breed, keeping readers abreast of what is happening within the breed. There are numerous articles on dogs in general by well-seasoned breeders.

Exhibitors and judges and, most important of all, the forthcoming shows are listed. This is where you will be able to see where and when shows are being held and who to apply to for entry forms. When the entry form for the show arrives, read it carefully. Take note of the closing date, check the classification and decide on the class best suited for your pup. It may be worth having a word with his breeder before filling in the entry form. If possible, have someone who shows regularly check that you have completed it correctly. Post back well before the closing date arrives.

Travel and the distance to shows need to be considered when entering a show. If it is a particularly long way to travel it might be worth considering travelling with a fellow exhibitor, then the driving and the fuel costs can be shared. It is good to attend your first few shows with a seasoned exhibitor, for they will know the location of the show, the time it takes to arrive there, and what the traffic situation is usually like getting into the show. Quite often they will know the layout of the show ground and where it is best to park in relation to getting dogs and dog gear to your marquee. It is important to arrive early enough to get yourself and your dog settled into your location without any undue hassle and harassment; you both need to be calm and collected and free of stress.

Remember the tension you feel will go

The Shiba must learn to stand still during the judge's examination.

The judge will check the mouth for full dentition, and the correct scissor bite.

The coat will be assessed to ensure it has the correct outer coat and undercoat.

Photos: John Daniels.

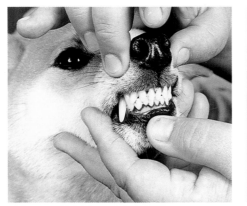

down the lead to the dog. If it is the pup's first time at a benched show, it is a good idea to take along a family member who can stay with the pup on the bench if and when you need to be away. This will give the puppy the confidence and comfort to cope with the strange surroundings. If you are able to take along his vari-crate for the bench, that is better still, for he knows this is his place of safety and security.

Your dog's grooming is a daily task. Working towards having him in tip-top condition for showing is a continuous process. It is sensible to have prepared your dog bag the day before the show, with the items you will need at the show. These include a show lead and collar, a bench chain and collar (if used), brushes, combs and grooming preparations, a water bowl, a Ring Card clip or armband, scissors, and a travelling box and bedding or a vari-crate.

Once you have settled your dog down it is important to purchase a show catalogue; this will detail what time you can expect to be in the ring. The dogs entered for competition are all listed in this. It will give you a list of the breeds attending and which classes the dogs are entered in. Once you have checked that your entry details are correct, you can relax. You may need to give your exhibit a final grooming before he enters the ring, so be sure to give yourself plenty of time for this.

SENSIBLE ASSESSMENTS

As you become a seasoned show-goer you meet and make many friends, but unfortunately you will also possibly make a few enemies. There will always be the people who seem unable to make an honest assessment of their own dogs, and those who are kennel-blind – in other words, if they have not bred the dog then it is no good! It is a sad part of the dog world but, as in all competition, it is inevitable. It is useful to listen, to select, and to learn to disregard what you do not find applicable or suitable to you. No-one, no matter who, knows it all! We all, even after many many years in dogs, are still learning, and that is part of the pleasure of owning dogs.

If you *do* ask for an opinion, do not be upset if what you are told is not what you want to hear. Hopefully, you are being given an honest assessment of your dog. We all know our own dog's failings, or we should do, and can only hope their good points outweigh the bad. Some breeders like to think that all the dogs that come from their kennels are of show quality but this is, of course, a physical impossibility. You should be honest about the quality of your Shiba. We should all be objective about our stock, for, at the end of the day, no one wants

to be showing inferior dogs. Showing is a costly exercise both in time and money, and competition is fierce. You need to know that your exhibit is at the very least up to the standard of the other exhibits – and better if possible.

You need to be able to go into the ring with confidence in your dog and your ability to get the most out of him, for the exhibitor with a poor dog is not going to enjoy the pleasure and rewards that a successful showing gives. Dogs as well as humans have good days as well as bad days. Some days your Shiba is totally with you and another day he is totally out of tune with you. It is a fact of life and there is little you can do about it. But just remember, win or lose, the dog you arrived with at the show in the morning, the one you know and love, is the same one you are taking home that night. And there is always tomorrow.

SHOW TRAVEL

Shibas generally travel well. If you are unfortunate enough to have one that travels badly it can make showing difficult and sometimes impossible, for you cannot expect the Shiba to arrive at a show and go happily into the ring if he has been traumatised throughout the journey.

Your Shiba should be introduced to the car when he is just a few weeks old. Short journeys, accompanied on the back seat by a family member, should be his first introduction to the car. Then go for longer journeys followed by pleasurable experiences, a romp in the park or on the beach or a walk through the woods, always accompanied with cuddles and shows of affection, so they become excursions that he looks forward to. He will also be pleased at the signs of the family getting ready for a trip in the car, knowing that he is being taken along as well – after all he is a family member too, and should always be considered in this light.

Long journeys for the exhibitor, as well as the exhibit, can be very tiring and sometimes neither of you feel at your best, so sometimes arriving at a show site the day or night before can be the answer. It then gives both of you the time to collect yourselves and settle before the big day arrives. Our show schedules are worked around our annual holiday. With a caravan in tow we make the most of our show days and holidays at the same time. In good company what more can you ask? After a long day's showing, a social evening with friends and exhibitors, putting the day's judging to rights before setting off for home the next day, is just perfect.

HOW TO A SHOW A JAPANESE DOG

The handler should stand behind the dog with the lead on the lower part of the dog's neck held loosely at a 45-degree angle. The dog should look straight ahead, standing naturally and positively. Showing the dog on a tight lead will cause wrinkles on the head and face and make the ears appear wider. It will also pull the eyes up to an incorrect angle. Stringing up a dog while on the move will cause him to tighten up and lose his natural flow and strong powerful gait. Baiting the dog is not allowed. Baiting is when the handler has a morsel or tidbit in his hand to tempt the dog and to gain the dog's attention, thus getting him to stand foursquare and alert. Usually the

handler stands in front of the dog to do this. Baiting can also be done from outside the ring, not by using a treat or morsel, but by attracting the dog's attention. This is usually done by a family member clapping or calling the dog's name from the ringside. The effect is that the dog stands alert and interested. In Japan, quite often two dogs will do a 'stand-off', which means that they placed face-to-face a short distance apart. They are expected to 'face-off' each other and the dog that looks away, or is less confident, or who shows timidity, is discounted.

BECOMING A SHOW JUDGE

Once hooked by the Shiba, your involvement with the breed will escalate and widen. You will quickly wish to add to your stock, whether by purchasing another dog from a breeder or perhaps by breeding your own puppy. Possibly, after the passage of time, with much learning and participation in breed activities you will, if you have shown your Shiba, decide that you are ready for the responsibility of judging the breed. This is not an exercise you should take on lightly, for the future of the breed can be affected.

As you get your 'eye in' on the breed your responsibilities for pursuing the characteristics and conformation according to the Breed Standard are extremely important. Of course, no dog is perfect, they all have their good and their bad points. Weighing up those different aspects in the show ring, with perhaps only two or three minutes of time being allowed for a close examination of each dog, and in the remainder of the time having to assess the dog's movement and deportment, becomes quite an arduous task, and not one that should be undertaken without several years involvement with the breed. The dog, while being visually close to the Breed Standard, should also be sound in mind and body.

HAVING AN 'EYE' FOR A DOG

You will, when showing your dog, want the opinion of the expert, and the confirmation of other people in the breed that your dog is a worthy specimen. In theory this should mean that he conforms closely to the Standard and should perpetuate and improve the breed. In practice there are many other factors that creep into the equation. Having an 'eye' for a good dog is something that some people are born with, thus making them good judges. It is, nevertheless, after numerous years of involvement with dogs, possible to acquire an 'eye' for a dog.

Having bred good dogs does not automatically mean you can judge them. Conversely, having an 'eye' for a good dog does not necessarily mean that you can breed one. Knowing what to look for in construction and conformation is something that you learn through experience with that breed. It is important to select dogs that are visual representatives of their breed. Having studied the Standard for the breed thoroughly, and made careful note of the unacceptable points or faults stipulated, you have then the by-no-means easy task of weighing up the good points against the bad. Bad points that can harm the breed have to be considered carefully and not be perpetuated.

THE OBJECTIVE JUDGE

Sadly, the outcome of the show ring can influence people in their breeding programmes, even though, from the distance of the ringside, those people are not able to determine such important aspects as the mouth of the dog, the coat texture or even the dog's temperament. It is your honesty and integrity that is on the line. In order to be a good judge, you must be totally objective. The dog in front of you should be all that is being considered when you are judging; there is no room for politics in the dog scene. People's likes and dislikes, views and fancies are irrelevant; only the dog is of concern, or should be, while you are judging. You owe it to the breed to be honest. You do not owe favours to people, only to the breed. It does not matter who bred the dog; if it is a good representative of the breed, that is all that matters.

In the ring, as a judge, you should carry a blueprint in your mind of the dog that fits the Breed Standard. You are not there to judge to 'your' type of Shiba or 'their' type of Shiba, only to the Japanese Standard Type of Shiba. The more you judge, hopefully, the better and more experienced you become. People do appreciate a judge with integrity. Whether they agree with your decisions or not, if you judge honestly, without fear or favour, there is little else that can be asked of you. Remember, you cannot and will not please all the people all the time. So long as you have judged as you see fit, and you know the reasons for your selections, then you are able to answer any criticism that may come .

As I have said, dogs are like humans – some days they are on top of the world

Crufts 1994: The author judging in traditional Japanese costume.

and some days they are off form. You can only judge the dogs on the day and you should not allow previous results to colour your judgement. Being in the show ring should be a happy and pleasurable experience for both dogs and handlers.

DECORUM IN THE RING

As the judge you must conduct yourself with decorum. Dressing correctly is important. While being smart, you must also wear something that is functional. High-heel shoes are impractical, whether the venue is inside or out. The weather must be considered if the judging is to take place outside. Clothes that are flowing or cumbersome should be avoided, as they sometimes distract the dogs. Conduct yourself with patience and gentleness. If the dog is being difficult, as only a Shiba knows how, be patient, give his handler time to settle him.

Approach from the front, never from

behind. Let the dog see you coming, he is then prepared for your examination. Handle him gently, no roughness, for many a young dog has been put off shows by an initial rough handling by a judge. Let the handler show you his teeth, the front first and then each side in turn. It is neither necessary or healthy for you to put your hands into the mouth of each of the dogs in turn. Apart from the risk of passing on any infections, the dog will be happier to have his mouth probed by his handler than by a stranger.

You should give every dog the same amount of time and attention. The owner/handlers have all paid their fees to have you go over their dogs and give an honest assessment, whether or not a glance has already told you that the dog falls short of the breed's visual requirements. The dogs should be praised and loved, for they have done their best for you and a kindly word costs nothing, and does put them at their ease.

While you are comparing the dogs in the ring, you should also be comparing them to the Breed Standard. They are in competition with each other as to who is closest to the Breed Standard. You may get a perfectly behaved Shiba who shows his heart out alongside another who, though not so well-behaved, is closer to the Standard. The unsettled one should be recognised for his qualities, for he will improve in behaviour the more he is shown, but the one lacking in breed characteristics may never develop the breed requirements fully. It is important that you give every dog the benefit of your knowledge and your experience on the day.

HOW TO JUDGE

The overall profile of the dog is what you consider initially, viewed from front and then from both sides, and finally from the rear. In profile he should look compact and be proportionally balanced, with well-developed muscle tone. He should be of correct height and length. His head shape should be that of a blunt triangle. His neck should be well arched and strong, reaching into a level top-line and finishing with a correct tail carriage. His coat colour should be clear and pristine. He should be standing four-square and confident.

Viewed from the front he should stand parallel, with feet turning neither in nor out. He should not stand wide, his chest should be deep (viewed from the side it should reach to his elbows). On closer examination his head and expression are the first considerations. The male should be masculine in head, while the female should have a feminine appearance. The Shiba should have a calm steady gaze, from dark almond eyes. His ear set should give a hooded effect in profile, be thick in substance, and rounded at the tip and wide at the base. The lowest base of the ear should be in line with the tip of the eye. The eye set should be almond-shaped (tipping slightly at the corners) with dark irises. The cheeks should be full. The teeth should be a full dentition with correct scissors bite. Missing teeth should be penalised.

Top-line, tuck-up and rear angulation are next to be considered. The Shiba should have only a moderate tuck-up and moderate angulation. His topline should be level, with no dipping behind the withers. The coat texture should be plush to the eye and harsh to the touch, with a soft undercoat, with slightly longer outer coat and be of good quality. The tail should be of reasonable length, set correctly on the back and lying with the curl to one side. Legs should be sturdy, with good bone and strong, cat-like feet, and the nails should be dark.

To be noted is his temperament while you examine him. Does he stand firm, confident and aware? Once close examination has been completed, he should then be moved out from you and then back again. He should be alert, brisk and positive in his movement; there should be no throwing out of his feet as he comes forward, he should move parallel. Going away from you there should be no hocking. On his return to you, he should stand with confidence, be noble and look assertive.

Thus each dog in turn is gone over, and a note made of his conformity to the Standard. Finally you will assess and select your line-up, pulling out your selection in order of placings, first place through to fifth place. You will be expected to do a critique on each of your placings and this should be done at this time. Your critique should be fair, honest and without malice.

6 TRAINING SHOW JUDGES

The criteria for becoming a judge vary greatly from country to country. This chapter illustrates how stringent some of the training is, particularly in Japan where the protection of the Japanese dogs such as the Shiba Inu is of paramount importance.

TRAINING TO BE A JUDGE IN JAPAN

In Japan there are regulations laid down specifically for judges, trainees and judges' assistants. Judging dogs in Japan is considered to be a very great honour and many years of experience are required, as well as the completion of the learning programmes and the examinations. The Nihon Ken Hozonkai (NIPPO) is composed of Chapters and Headquarters. The Chapters have to be chartered – that is, licensed. A recent Shiba Year Book listed eight regional groups and forty-nine Chapters. Each Chapter puts on its own show and, in addition, Headquarters has the National Shows. The procedures for being accepted as a qualified judge in Japan are very comprehensive and give a thorough judging apprenticeship – one that we all might envy!

Judge Trainees are nominated by the Judges' Department from among the qualified Judges' Assistants. The number of Judge Trainees nominated by the Judges' Department at any one time is normally forty. However, vacancies can be filled whenever necessary. During the nomination period Judge Trainees must continue to carry out the business affairs of Judges' Assistants, and they must attend the Training Academy given by the Judges' Department, and take the lectures as well as the prescribed examination. Judge Trainees must serve as a Judge at least four times, they must attend the Training Academy at least twice, and must pass the prescribed examination. From the time of accepting the nomination of the Judges' Department, it is a full three years. When duties are neglected without cause, or when the Judges' Department determines unfitness, one can be dismissed, even if the nomination period has not expired.

The conditions for Judges' Trainees also apply to Judges' Assistants. Each Chapter recommends qualified people from among its membership to the Judges' Department. Those in the position of Judges' Assistant help with the execution of the duties of the Judge in charge at the Chapter Shows. However, they do not have a voice in the judgement.

After accepting the nomination of the Chapter, the Judges' Assistants are in office at least two years: if they have not performed the duties of their position at least four times they have not met the selection requirements for Judges' Assistant. Judges' Assistants must have been members for at least five years of a particular Chapter. They must have a reliable character and be co-operative with the Chapter administration. They should have an enthusiasm for the Japanese dog and experience in breeding and raising them. They should not be dog merchants, or anything related to that. The total number of Chapter nominations is not exact, and it is limited to the number required as assistants to the judge in charge at the Chapter shows.

The term of Judges' Assistants is a full three years from the acceptance of the Chapter nomination. However, the Chapter is not prevented from re-nominating. If duties are neglected without cause, or the Chapter makes a determination of incompetence, the nomination can be amended and the application to the Judges' Department revoked, even if the term has not expired.

To verify the performance of the office of Judges' Assistant, the Chapter submits a catalogue of show results, stating the surname of the Judges' Assistant who has worked at the show, and the Judge in charge confirms it.

JUDGING IN THE UK

In the UK the Breed Clubs have Judges Lists, from which a judge can be selected. However, the format for collating these lists is wide and variable. Some Breed Clubs hold judges' assessment days, or learning days for new judges who can take the opportunity to understand and to appreciate the finer points of their chosen breed. The more established Breed Clubs have weekend teach-ins, with a test paper at the end of the session. A certain standard has to be reached before a would-be judge can appear on a Club's judging list. There are usually three levels of judging lists.

An A List contains the names of judges approved for officiating at Championship level, with the ability to award Challenge Certificates. It also contains the names of those judges with the ability to judge Groups and Best in Shows. A B List contains the names of judges approved for officiating at Open Show level, and a C list is for newly-recognised judges who have yet to qualify as having fulfilled the required number of judging appointments in order to appear on the B List. Judging at a Breed Open Show is invaluable if an aspiring judge wishes to appear on the A List.

A prospective trainee judge will have been in the breed for several years. He or she will have bred several litters and have exhibited successfully in the show ring. Local Club Matches are a good beginning for the aspiring judge, who then gradually progresses on to judging at Open Shows. Many Breed Clubs require that a would-be judge should have adjudicated at an Open Show, with classes for the Breed, at least seventy times, and to have judged at least two hundred dogs of the breed. They will be expected to have bred at least one Champion dog and to have owned the breed for a minimum of five years before they are considered for inclusion in a Championship Show List. Having owned, bred and judged other breeds of dogs can help but, while this background is invaluable, there is no short cut to learning and recognising the important traits required by specific breeds such as the Shiba.

When Show secretaries and committees are selecting judges for their shows they have the relevant Breed Clubs' judging lists to refer to. When their selection has been made, those judges are contacted to ascertain their availability. When this information has been received, the secretaries then contact the Kennel Club for its approval of the judges selected. The Breed Clubs can select the judges, but the Kennel Club has the final say in all judging appointments.

In the UK there is a Diploma Course which is extremely comprehensive and takes about a year to eighteen months to complete. Places on the course are sought after, and a Pass is very beneficial to a would-be judge.

The Japanese Shiba Inu Club of Great Britain's format for their judging list is as follows: Overseas judges are invited at the discretion of the Committee. Then there is the A List. For inclusion on the A2 List, judges must have taken the Club's Assessment. At least 50 per cent

of the final Assessment mark must be achieved from the assessment and placing of the dogs. Candidates must have achieved a pass mark of 75 per cent or above, or have taken the Assessment and have judged 50 Breed classes, which must have included two Championship shows or one Club show and 100 seen Shiba Inus.

All would-be judges on the B List must have taken the Assessment. At least 50 per cent of the final Assessment mark must have been achieved from the assessment and placing of the dogs. Candidates must have attained a pass mark of 50 to 74 per cent, or a pass mark of 30 per cent or above and also have taken the Assessment and judged 20 Breed classes and 50 seen Shiba Inus.

All on the C List must have taken the Assessment. At least 50 per cent of the final Assessment mark must be achieved from the Assessment and the placings of the dogs. This list is for those who, in the opinion of the Committee based on the Assessor's report, need a little more experience of the breed. The minimum Assessment pass mark is 25 per cent.

Promotion or deletion from the Judges List is dependent upon the opinion of the Committee, based on the Assessor's report. It is also based upon written praise or criticism submitted to the Committee for consideration when the list is revised annually before its presentation to the Annual General Meeting. Successful Candidates will be placed no higher than the B List until their capabilities have been assessed and they have fulfilled all the criteria.

ALLOCATIONS OF CCs
Once a breed has been recognised by the

Kennel Club and Challenge Certificates are to be awarded, the Breed Club is given four representative shows for their first set of certificates. These are at Crufts, the Birmingham Dog Show Society, the Scottish Kennel Club and the Welsh Kennel Club. CCs may also be allocated to other shows by the General Committee on application from the Show Societies. However, allocations of CCs are discretionary and conditional upon Show Societies being able to prove that they have previously run satisfactory shows.

At shows where more than one breed is scheduled, there must be at least eight classes for breeds for which Challenge Certificates are on offer, and an Open and a Limit Class for each sex must be provided. The selection of the judges must be in accordance with the rules of the Show Society and names must be submitted for approval to the General Committee at the Kennel Club, together with evidence in support of the application if this is required by the General Committee.

There must be an interval of *not less than 12 months* between any judge awarding CCs to the same sex of the same breed. All applications for the approval to judge must be lodged at the Kennel Club, with the Secretary, by the Show Society, at least 12 months prior to the show date, on a form that is provided by the Kennel Club.

JUDGING IN THE US

The American Kennel Club has strict requirements for anyone considering applying to be a judge. They must have had ten years experience in dogs and have the documents to prove it, such as the dates of litters, records of exhibiting at shows and club membership. They must have owned or exhibited several dogs of the initial breed they wish to judge, and be able to document considerable experience in the majority of the remaining breeds in which they are requesting to judge. They must have bred and raised at least four litters in any one breed and have produced two Champions out of a minimum of four litters, whether or not the applicant owned or handled them. They must have had five stewarding assignments at AKC member or licensed shows and have judged six AKC sanctioned matches, sweepstakes or futurities – fun matches, junior showmanship or Obedience assignments are not acceptable. And they must meet the occupational eligibility requirements under AKC Rules.

Once the AKC has accepted and approved an application, the candidate must then pass a comprehensive examination to demonstrate their understanding of the AKC Rules, Policies and Judging procedures and pass a written test on the Standard of each breed for which they have been approved. Then there is an interview, so that the applicant can personally demonstrate their breed knowledge and qualifications, and there is an 'open book' examination on canine terminology, conformation and anatomy.

Successful applications are then submitted to the Staff Committee and Board Liaison for review and action. Applicants provisionally approved for breeds are notified in writing and their names are published twice in the *Gazette*. After five provisional assignments in each breed, the applicant notifies the Judges

Department in writing and requests regular approval. The application is evaluated by the Staff Committee and Board Liaison, applicants are notified of the decision and their names are published in the *Gazette*. Unsuccessful applicants must wait one year from the Board date before submitting another application.

We can see from this that every effort is made to ensure that people wishing to judge have a thorough background in dogs.

JUDGING ON THE CONTINENT
In Scandinavia a potential judge must, first of all, have been a competent and independent ring secretary and ring steward and have carried out these duties many times. The demands made on them are very much more stringent than in the UK. The ring secretaries and stewards must be fully conversant with the rules and regulations. They must have a complete knowledge and understanding of the judging and grading system. They need to know which dog is eligible for which award. The secretaries need to be able to transcribe detailed dictated critiques in the judge's native language. There is a great deal of paperwork involved for the ring staff, while the training they are receiving will benefit them in their efforts to become good judges. A daily rate is paid to the trainees, along with free accommodation and travelling expenses.

First-time judges on the continent should be between 25 and 55 years of age, and have a good working knowledge of English. They should have the backing of their respective Breed clubs. In Sweden new judges are required to attend a three-day seminar, which covers anatomy, judging techniques, behaviour, Kennel Club rules, gait and movement, coat and general breed type. The teachers are usually well-established all-rounder judges, vets, and other experts in their chosen fields. An examination is taken at the end of the course and an 80 per cent pass rate is required. Failed candidates are able to re-apply and take the examination again the following year.

When the candidate has passed the exams they are called in for an informal interview at the Kennel Club. The interviewers are usually senior dog people. The Kennel Club's aim is to ascertain the potential and the attitude of the candidate, for they need to be good and competent judges when representing the Kennel Club. The standard requirements are very high and of some 70 people applying recently to become judges only 17 reached the next stage, which is the Preparation Course.

THE PREPARATION COURSE
This takes place with around 16 people living-in and attending the course for seven days. The candidates arrive on Sunday and the following week is very intensive, with classes starting around 8:00 am and finishing at 7:00 pm. The candidates live, eat, breathe and sleep dogs for the duration of the course. There are four, highly experienced breeders, each with knowledge of several breeds of dogs. They will each have a 'ring' and a group of four of the participating candidates. Each day the group changes and moves on to the next judge, until they have studied under each in turn. A number of dogs will have been

asked to attend at various times.

The students will not necessarily only have the breed of their choice to evaluate, but they will have others as well, thus giving them a broad basis of anatomy, movement, coats, trimming and grooming and measuring, if and when necessary. Though each day there are lectures, most of the time is taken up with assessment and learning within the rings, giving the participants the opportunity of looking at, and going over, dogs and then making their evaluation. This is done at a general level. The candidates highlight the dogs' good and bad points. Getting into the finer breed points is not encouraged at this time. The ability to recognise a good or bad specimen, whatever the breed – having an 'eye' for a dog, in other words – is what the examining judges are looking for. Studying the dog's movement and explaining why it moves as it does, helps the student and makes him consider the dog's actual structure, and what to look for when assessing a dog in general terms.

Many dogs later, the examiners will report on the candidate's overall ability and whether or not he should proceed further. Many other facts will also have been taken note of, for example how the candidate handles the dogs and the dogs' handlers, and how the candidate relates to the ring staff. How did the candidate conduct himself in the ring? Was he appropriately dressed? How did he handle a tricky situation or dog? Did he keep his composure? Did he work too slowly or too fast?

Of course, the candidates will be nervous, aware of being watched and assessed. At the end of the course the teachers and examiners are there to evaluate the students and to give them help, knowledge and support towards their goal of becoming a competent and respected judge.

The students have to be able to give a comprehensive and informative critique on each dog, outlining his virtues and his faults. When an exhibitor has spent a large amount on entering a show, they have done this because they wish to know what the judge thinks about their particular dog compared to the rest of the competition. It is important that the judge can concisely explain to the exhibitor his reasons for his placings on the day.

SPECIALISATION
For those completing this course successfully the work has only just begun. Now comes the task of achieving their goal in their chosen breed. The Breed Standard has to be known and understood thoroughly. The finer points of the breed must be appreciated, recognised and understood. It is at this time that the candidate is able to act as a student judge alongside a judge at a show. The student is there to learn, to observe and to listen to the judge, who will ask him questions as the day progresses. The student must accompany three different judges on three different occasions. When the student is in the ring with a judge, there is a sign displayed by the ring side to explain that a student judge is in attendance, so that the exhibitors and ringside onlookers are not confused.

On being passed suitable by three judges, the student can apply to become a trainee judge. A trainee judge accompanies two further judges in the ring, but this time he is allowed to go over the dogs, and watch the dogs move, and then write up a critique and grading without any reference to the judge present. This takes place at a licensed show. The trainee judge must complete his critique and grading before the judge does his, so there is no possibility of him being influenced. The judge will study the trainee's report.

While they do not have to agree on all of the placings, the trainee must be able to justify his reasons for his placings. The judge will ascertain the trainee's abilities and reasons, and finally sign the appropriate forms if he feels the trainee is ready to judge. The Kennel Club will then probably approve the trainee to judge in his own right.

Once the Kennel Club's approval to judge in a chosen breed has been received, a judge can then apply to other Breed clubs, stating the reasons why he would like to judge their breed, and his judging experience to date in other breeds. If the Club is in agreement, the would-be judge will have to take another exam run by the Kennel Club for that particular breed. The exams are run every six months or so. The exam requires the judging of between five to eight dogs of the breed, with breed specialists acting as the examiners. The candidate has to give a verbal critique, and grade and place all of the dogs. The examiners will then discuss the candidate's abilities and then award either a pass or a fail. Anyone failing can re-apply, but failure to pass on the second attempt means that the would-be judge cannot apply again for five years.

7 *THE VERSATILE SHIBA INU*

While the Shiba is only really true to himself, once he has forged a special bond with his own special person he can become accommodating and pliable in performing most of the tasks that other breeds pursue. His wish to please his special person is boundless. Because of his versatility he can, if he wishes, attune himself to just about anything – Agility, Obedience, Hunting and even, when necessary, to becoming a therapy dog.

THERAPY DOGS
A therapy is a *visiting* companion dog, a dog that visits old and infirm people in hospitals, in nursing homes, and in their own homes. Many of these elderly sick people have had to part with their own beloved pets when they have to be taken into hospitals and nursing homes for treatment or for permanent stays. The wrench of leaving their animals, together with the move into a strange place, can be very traumatic for the sick and the elderly. It has been found that allowing a dog in to visit the sick has helped patients to adjust and to make a quicker

recovery. The therapeutic effect has been remarkable. However, the visiting dog needs to be stable, to enjoy meeting people and to accept fondling and caressing. We all know how beneficial it is just to have a dog sit by you and allow you to pat and stroke him. Dogs have no hang-ups about the sick and the elderly; all they ask is that they are handled gently. To have a dog visit regularly and to stay for an hour or so, a dog that can be talked to, played with and cuddled, is very relaxing. The owner/handler is always there to accompany the dog. Shibas make excellent therapy dogs.

OBEDIENCE
Shibas do enjoy Obedience once they have begun to have some success at it. Joining an Obedience Club may seem foreign to many Shiba owners, for their initial reaction will be "but my Shiba does not have the patience or the natural ability to do Sits, Down Stays or walk to heel off the lead." In fact, the opposite is, in truth, the case.
    Many Shibas do Obedience and achieve very good results, competing

along with many other breeds. The relationship between the handler and dog becomes much closer, and both of them work together in harmony and even compete with each other. The dog respects the handler and the handler respects the dog, for it means they have to work hard together to attain their goals.

There is a strong desire in people and in animals to learn and to achieve success. Proving worth in ourselves and gaining respect from others is something we all enjoy and are happy to strive for. In animals the wish to please and to be praised is very strong. We all need challenges to keep us motivated and 'on the ball'. Dogs are no different; they need challenges and new experiences to keep them motivated and fulfilled. It is not unusual to find that the greater the challenge, the more one enjoys achieving the impossible. Given the Shiba and his uniqueness, there is no greater challenge! Most Shibas, male and female, have the Alpha streak in them – 'I'm Number One'. Given this attitude, Obedience is a must, not an option.

The Shiba's general assertiveness when among other dogs, or when confronted by another dog, is something that has to be anticipated and controlled, without the dog being aware that you are doing it. Early enrolment in basic training classes is the answer; getting used to other dogs milling around and being in close proximity is the start. Learning to Sit, Stay and Come on command, again with other dogs around, is good early grounding. As you build up to more difficult challenges, the Shiba seems to thrive and enjoy it. The harder the task, the more rewarding it seems to be for him.

COPING WITH AGGRESSION

Aggression towards other dogs has to be overcome right from the beginning. Many years ago, when we had Rottweilers, we learned several different ways of overcoming this. Fortunately the Rottweiler gives you numerous indications when he is seriously considering chastising another dog. Either it is in the way that he stiffens and grows taller, or the way his eyes get

The intelligent Shiba Inu can be trained to perform a variety of tasks.

Photos: John Daniels.

darker and blacker, or even the rumble that starts way down in his boots and gradually rises to his throat. But forewarned is forearmed. Once you have learnt to read the signs, you are prepared to act before he does.

Rottweilers can be particularly protective when in the car. If someone drives up close to you and tail-gates, or a motor-biker is tailing you, the Rottweiler can, and will, show his disapproval. A passenger sitting alongside the dog with a plastic squeegee bottle full of water can be very effective. When the dog is about to roar his disapproval at the intruder, a firm but loud No and a quick squirt in the dog's face will stop this behaviour. You may need to do this on a few occasions, but the dog learns very quickly the error of his ways.

When you are in close proximity to other dogs, similar devices can be used. A squirt into the dog's mouth of something unpleasant, like lemon juice, followed by a shake and a loud No has the desired effect. The dog very quickly associates the unpleasant taste with his aggressive reaction and begins to realise that his behaviour is not acceptable and will not be tolerated.

AGILITY AND THE SHIBA

The Shiba in hunting mode has to be agile and quick when chasing small quarry and birds. This requires being able to move through the terrain nimbly and sure-footedly. Most breeds of dogs are happiest when they are doing what comes naturally. Working Agility is a competitive event that allows dog and man to compete in a fun activity using the following equipment and obstacles.

Weave Poles A series of upright poles spaced apart that the dog has to negotiate in an 'in and out' pattern, passing left at the first pole, right at the second, left at the third, and so on.

Jumps There are numerous different types of jumps – hoop jumps, brush jumps, and jumps set at different heights.

Tunnels Some are straight, with light at the end. Some tunnels have collapsed cloth sections that the dog must nuzzle his way through to the end.

The Dogwalk a balance beam about 12 to 18 inches from the floor that the dog has to walk across, with a ramp up to it at one end, and down from it at the other.

The A Frame This is two wood sections joined by hinges down the middle so that it can be set up at different angles and heights. The dog jumps or scales up to the top of the first section and down the other side.

AGILITY
Photos: John Daniels.

LEFT: *Negotiating the weave poles.*

BELOW: *The Shiba is agile and quick and clearly enjoys the sport of agility.*

On the dogwalk.

Through the tyre.

At the top of the A Frame.

Many other obstacles can be set up, usually due to the ingenuity of the trainers, and there are also seesaws and slides. The start and finish of the obstacle course can be a table top where the dog remains until it is released.

To begin with the dog has to be introduced to each obstacle in turn, to become familiar with it and to learn to negotiate it correctly. He then has to learn the correct order in which to tackle the obstacles. Ultimately he will, once released on the start, go around the course at great speed, while his handler just stands in the middle, praising him and encouraging him on. The fun and enjoyment experienced by the dog is very apparent when you watch his carefree abandon as he flies around the course off the lead.

As with all training, I believe in reward and praise. I use food treats as rewards for the dog who achieves. Allowing your dog to watch other experienced Agility working dogs on the equipment is quite often all that is needed to entice the Shiba to have a go, for he will not want to be outdone or to be missing out on the fun. Shibas have a naturally inquisitive and enquiring mind and their love of heights and of looking down on others is a great bonus. Skill in climbing without any obvious footholds is another natural instinct which the Shiba possesses. He also seems to be able to jump from a standing still position, and the height he gains is unbelievable.

THE HUNTING SHIBA
Although they are natural hunters, a relic from their feral days, not all Shibas are necessarily good hunters, but in the hands of an experienced trainer the Shiba's capabilities are boundless. There was a Red Shiba male named Hamawaku Go who hunted birds with his owner Takahashi Hideo. On their first hunt, in 1966 they returned with over 50 mountain birds. During their second hunting season, in 1967, Hamawaku took up the scent of a bear's cave some 400 feet away from him. Rushing to the cave he lured the bear out and the hunter took aim and bagged it. Hamawaku had entered the cave without hesitation and confronted the bear – a 20 pound dog confronting a 270 pound male bear! It was in February 1968 that Hamawaku caught the scent of another bear. The snows were particularly heavy and he had to wait for his master to arrive. Then he jumped onto his master's shoulders and up into the mouth of the cave where the bear was hibernating. Once again he lured the bear out for his master to shoot. Hamawaku was then three and a half years old.

There are many tales of the Shiba and his hunting prowess. Shibas can, and frequently do, out-run rabbits, returning with their prize in their mouths for your approval. In their native Japan, on the mountains, in the forests and on the wild plains, the Shiba hunted pheasant, wild duck and various other game birds. His skills were also used for hunting foxes and racoons, along with other small quarry. He loves to be included in hunting trips and his courage is undeniable.

Accompanying the family on weekend hikes into the hills and mountains becomes an adventure for all. Packing the car up with the camping equipment and provisions immediately signals to the Shiba that there is adventure ahead. They become restless and fidgety and will not be still until they have been placed in the back of the car ready for the journey.

Their delight in returning to their roots is obvious when they fly off into the undergrowth and pursue their games of hide-and-seek and tag, with a broad grin on their faces as they return to you, just to make sure you are keeping up with them and their antics. The taller the grass, the better, for then they have to leap to keep an eye on each other's whereabouts – it is all part of their hunting games.

Frequently the Shiba, when out on a trek, will get the scent of another animal, be it alive or dead, and off he will go, returning with some capture or other. Shibas seem to have their own on-board radar system which rarely lets them down. One minute they are by your side, ambling along enjoying the countryside, and the next they have taken off at full speed on a seek and retrieve mission. The trek then becomes a hunt. However, once the hunt is over and they have let off steam, they will then stay fairly close to you for the rest of the hike, usually circling you, but still racing and chasing about and covering many miles in the course of a day. They enjoy and seem able to sustain themselves in most climates, whether hot or cold. Snow seems to hold a special fascination for the Shiba. They love to dig holes in it and, especially when it is deep, they enjoy bounding through it. They are not so keen on water and they seem loath to submerge entirely into it. Paddling is fine, but swimming is a very different consideration.

8 PRINCIPLES OF BREEDING

To breed or not to breed? This is a decision not to be taken lightly. Why do you think you should breed? Surely not for the old adage that every bitch should have at least one litter. Let us put that old myth to rest once and for all, for there have been many bitches that have led happy, useful lives without having ever had a litter. Like some humans, some dogs are just not fit to have offspring. They are neither mentally or physically competent. However, with dogs we are at least able to look at their inherent faults and virtues and then make a decision.

We have a responsibility to our lovely Shibas. We have their future in our hands and we have a responsibility to breed Shibas that are true to type, with the distinct and unique characteristics, both physically and mentally, of their breed. We owe it to the Japanese people who have treasured and preserved this lovely breed over the centuries.

Mating and breeding your Shiba is a very serious subject. When you are considering it you have to bear one hundred per cent of the commitment and the decision-making. In nature's world the animal makes its own selection of a mate. In the scheme of things, only the fittest, with the necessary characteristics appertaining to their species, will survive and produce the next generation.

However, when you take on this decision, you decide who will be the sire and the dam, and what the future litter will be. What has gone before is history. You are now taking on the roll of perpetuator. What transpires from the resulting litter is your responsibility. You must accept it and deal with it. You should never get involved with breeding litters unless you are totally committed to the well-being, lifelong care and interest in the puppies you produce. This is an on-going process. Just because the puppies go off into new homes, this does not mean that your responsibility to them ends; having brought them into the world you owe it to them to be ever aware and concerned about them.

NOT A HOBBY FOR PET OWNERS
Breeding is a demanding and uncertain vocation. It is not a way of making a fast

buck. On the contrary, having a litter of puppies can and does cost you quite a lot of money. Remember that a stud fee has to be paid, suitable kennelling and whelping facilities bought, veterinary costs met, the in-whelp bitch's diet correctly maintained and the subsequent puppy diets arranged. Then there are registration fees, injections, heating and lighting costs, advertising fees and running on puppies that are not sold. If you are making money out of breeding, you must be doing something wrong.

It is cruel to bring unwanted puppies or unplanned puppies into the world. With hundreds of dogs being destroyed yearly, both pedigree and mongrels who, through no fault of their own, find themselves in pounds and kennels, we have a duty to ask ourselves whether this litter is really necessary. Can we guarantee the puppies caring and loving homes and, if the new home situation changes in a year or two down the road, are we able to take that dog back and either keep it or find it another suitable family?

SO WHY BREED?
You have a bitch, let us take stock of her. Why do you think you should be breeding from her? How closely does she fit the Shiba Standard? What has she to offer? Is she good enough to be breeding from? Does she have any defects? Is she a sound, typical specimen of the breed? Is her temperament sound enough for her to be a good mother? Have a word with the breeder from whom you purchased the bitch. Does she feel she is good enough to be bred from? I, personally, will only breed when I wish to keep a puppy myself.

When breeding you must be aiming to improve on what you have in your kennels. To improve on your stock should be your aim, always bearing in mind that the Standard is your blueprint and this is what you are aiming for at all times. Careful planning of your breeding programme is a must. Individual whims and fancies are not a responsible attitude in dog breeding. Anyone can breed a litter of puppies, but that will not benefit the breed and more likely it will be to the breed's detriment.

You need to be hypercritical of your stock. Is your bitch typical of the litter she came from – or was she the only outstanding one in the litter? Were her litter-mates also of good quality? What faults or hereditary problems have shown themselves in the litter she came from? What have the temperaments of the other puppies been like? Have any of them been bred from, or used at stud – if so, what were the resulting puppies like? Sometime you will get a 'flier' in a litter: this is a dog or bitch that has done outstandingly well in the show ring. Sometimes a pair of mediocre parents throw an otherwise outstanding specimen, but rarely does that 'flier' ever produce anything of note himself. Breeding from mediocre stock is risky and is it not worth taking the chance.

It is hard to look at the "light of your life" and be critical of his or her faults, or to know that there are proven hereditary faults, albeit that they may not always be visible. You may also know that other people are breeding from inferior dogs. But for your own peace of mind, and for the future of the breed, you must be determined not to perpetuate these problems.

THE ALPHA DOG

The Shiba Inu evolved over many centuries without the help of man, relying on the law of the wilds where the survival of the strongest and the fittest perpetuates the breed. Natural selection was the way. Unlike many man-made breeds, the Shiba is a product of its own making and so has many unique traits.

When man began to take a hand in the Shiba's future and survival, he took on the role of choosing the mate and the survival of the fittest became obsolete, as did the natural selection process. But we do still see today some of these past characteristics, though perhaps we do not always understand them. It is a fact that in a kennel of males and females there is always the alpha dog, the dog that the others respect and look up to. It manifests itself when a bitch comes into season and the other males seem to be totally oblivious of the fact, because they know that the alpha dog – the strongest and the fittest, as far as they are concerned – is around, and only the foolhardy will challenge him. This also occurs with bitches. When the alpha bitch is in evidence, other bitches seem to pass by their seasons without even showing any outward signs of having a season.

Because of their basic and close-to-nature characteristics, the Shiba is a package of contradictions. Just when you begin to think you are understanding them, they do something that is totally unexpected. All characteristics are hereditary, whether they are behavioural or visual. A look at the parents, and especially at the grandparents, should give you a good idea of what to expect of the puppies; not all the characteristics will be in every puppy but some characteristics will be in some puppies. Some characteristics seem to miss a generation, which is why I think it is important, if at all possible, to see the grandparents and great-grandparents.

As a breed develops in a country, we are able to build up a portfolio about what dog produces what, and where these characteristics come from. With the Shiba's origins having been in Japan, and given the vastness of the dog's ancestry, it has been doubly difficult, due to the language barrier, to catalogue this information so, for several generations, we are breeding in the dark. It is generally accepted that the last three generations showing on a pedigree are the most influential to any forthcoming litter; but, even so, characteristics can still come through from farther back on the pedigree from time to time. Knowing and seeing are your best and safest guides when planning a litter.

PREPARATIONS FOR BREEDING

Having decided that you do wish to breed your bitch, let us consider what else needs to be done before you go ahead. Has your bitch been hip X-rayed, eye-tested and patella-checked? These are all health checks that should be undertaken well in advance of your bitch coming into season. Hip X-rays are done once the Shiba reaches her first birthday (preferably not before) as the bones need time to grow and mature. Eyes can be tested much earlier and should be checked thereafter annually. Patellas can be checked from eight weeks of age onwards. The age at which you breed from your Shiba is debatable. In larger dogs breeders would not breed until the

When planning a mating, the pedigrees of both dog and bitch should be thoroughly researched.

female is two years of age or more. Many would not breed until a female has had her third season. With Shibas many consider that around a year old is fine; the Japanese consider that at the bitch's first season, which is usually at around nine or ten months of age, is best for her. However, it is the bitch's maturity which is the most important consideration before breeding and this varies from bitch to bitch. Maturity in both mind and body is paramount.

As with humans, dogs can vary enormously in their development. I have had a female have her first season as young as five months of age and I have heard of bitches not having a first season till they are sixteen months old. It is the same with maturity; some mature early and some are still not mentally stable until they are eighteen months or more.

Only you know your dog, and the responsibility is yours to decide when the time is right. Some females have seasons twice a year, some only once a year. Some go five or six months between seasons, others can go a year or fourteen months. As mentioned before, Shibas seem to be able to hide the fact that they are in season, and only a discerning and determined male will highlight the fact for you. So caution with your female, especially if there is a male around, is crucial. Keeping her in a secure environment is a must, just in case she decides to go walk-about with the first opportunist that comes along!

A female should only be bred from once a year; time must be given for her to recuperate after her litter, for having a litter of puppies takes quite a lot out of the female.

CHOOSING A STUD DOG

Having decided that you are going to breed from your bitch, you must once again assess her qualities and failures. What are her good points? Is she typical of the breed? What has she to offer as the dam? What, if anything, has she that you would not wish to reproduce? Where do her attributes come from? What are you aiming for in the forthcoming litter? Do you want puppies just like the dam, or have you a sire in mind that you particularly admire, or do you have something else in mind that you wish to produce?

Look at your bitch and be specific about her failings. For instance, does she have the correct tail-set, or is her tail a bit loose and does she carry it low? If so, be sure to choose a sire who has the correct tail-set, for choosing a male who has the same problem as your bitch will only 'stamp in' the unwanted trait. It may be that it is an inherent problem in that particular line, so extra caution needs to be taken to ensure you do not perpetuate the problem. Again, if in doubt, have a talk with the breeder of your bitch to clarify the point, as well as discussing your concerns with the owner of your chosen sire, for they will also not wish to have their dogs perhaps blamed for any shortcomings that may arise. It is only fair that you are honest with them. We insist on seeing the prospective dam before agreeing to the use of our stud dogs and, very occasionally, will refuse his service if we consider the female not to be suitable. We also always like to look at the bitch's pedigree to ascertain that there are no hidden problems in previous generations that, on the surface, are not obvious.

While your main concern is breeding to the Shiba Standard, there are many other aspects to consider when choosing a stud dog. Are you going to line-breed, out-cross or in-breed?

LINE-BREEDING

Line-breeding is the most favourable method. This is where the bitch and the dog have at least one common ancestor, usually in the first few generations of the pedigree. It can work well but it must be stressed that it all depends on the make-up of those involved. Line-breeding is important if you have not bred your bitch before, for this will give you some idea about what your bitch produces. Then at a later date you may need to out-cross to take your line on. Granddaughter to grandfather works well, as do half-brother to half-sister pairings. You are, of course, in time, going to have to use an out-crossed male to generate some new blood into your lines.

OUT-CROSSING

Out-cross breeding is where there are no related bloodlines in the first few generations. In other words, when you look at a pedigree you can see no names behind the bitch which are the same as the ones behind the dog. It is important that any out-cross male has been line-bred; otherwise, if he is also out-crossed, it could take several generations of breeding to be reasonably sure of what is actually there.

IN-BREEDING

In-breeding is another option, but not one that should be contemplated by the novice or inexperienced breeder. While it is a way of stamping your mark on the bloodlines, it is something that can have very negative consequences if you do not fully understand the genetics and breeding of the dogs behind your chosen partners. It can stamp in bad influences that take many years to clear from your lines, once having been established there.

NOVICE DOGS

There is a well-known saying that breeders have: it is 'If you like the dog, look at his sire'. In other words, it is the parents and grandparents of the dog you like that have produced the traits you see and admire and perhaps wish to perpetuate in your forthcoming litter but, remember, it takes 'two to tango' and your bitch will also have an influence in the resulting litter.

If this is the first mating of your bitch, it is preferable that the male has been used before, in other words that he is well-versed in the mating procedures. Two inexperienced dogs can cause nothing but problems for themselves and for their future use in breeding programmes, if their initial experience is a bad one. While I, personally, have found the Shiba to be a very resilient and confident animal in every aspect of mating, whelping and breeding, it is preferable to be aware of the possibility of problems when using novice dogs. If in doubt have an experienced breeder with you at the appropriate time.

STUD DOG TERMS

Having chosen your stud dog, you will need to book his use with his owners, giving them a rough idea as to when you think your female will be in season. It is usual for the bitch to go to the stud dog.

The distance you have to travel to the stud dog should be the least of the considerations when choosing a sire. Using the dog down the road, for no better reason than that he happens to be close at hand, is not something a caring and conscientious breeder would do. Likewise, a conscientious stud dog owner will not allow their dog to be used on just any bitch whose owner wishes it, without careful consideration of the bitch's worthiness to be bred from.

If the dog is a proven stud the owner will wish to be paid the stud fee at the time of mating. If the sire to be has not been proven then, usually, the stud fee is paid when the bitch is confirmed as being in whelp or when the puppies are born. All these options must be discussed at the time of contacting the stud dog's owner. Occasionally an agreement can be reached where, if you are not keeping a puppy yourself from your bitch, the stud's owner will take a puppy in lieu of the fee. Perhaps your bitch puppy was sold to you on the condition that the breeder takes back a pick of litter from her first litter. If this is the case, the breeder will quite often wish to choose the sire for that first litter. Whatever arrangements have been made, it is best to clarify all these options with the prospective stud-dog owner, so that they are fully in the picture.

I personally would advocate that you pay up-front when purchasing your original Shiba, and would advise that you do not get drawn into any commitments about your future litters. Many a friendship has fallen by the wayside through just such agreements not being honoured when the time comes. The same applies to stud fees – pay up and be done with them.

The question should also be addressed about what happens if your bitch has no puppies. Will you be able to use the sire again for free? Most owners will usually agree that their dog can be used again at the bitch's next season. What if only one puppy is born? Can you use the male again for free, or at a reduced rate? It is as well to remember that the stud fee is for the actual mating service and that, if no puppies result, it is not always the fault of the sire. Whatever arrangements are agreed, they should be in writing, with both parties holding a copy so that no misunderstandings occur at a later date.

The owner of the stud dog usually only allows one mating, but if a second is allowed, it is best to miss a day and then try again. Remember that the male's sperm will stay active for 24 hours at least once it is implanted in the female. If you have to travel a long distance to the male, this is something that should be considered when making your overnight arrangements.

The owners of stud dogs quite often insist that the bitch has a vaginal swab at the vet's before they are brought to their dogs. This is to ensure that bitch has no vaginal infection. It is something you should have done prior to her coming in season. If any infection is present, it will give you time for the vet to clear it up before she is mated. If undetected, it could result in problems in the whelps, who may be malformed.

TIMING THE MATING

Your bitch should be checked by your vet before mating; she should be up-to-date with her vaccinations, and a blood test should be taken to gauge her parvovirus immunity, which she will pass on to her litter. She should be wormed and, of course, be in good health for producing the forthcoming litter.

It is very important to keep a close eye on your Shiba when you know she is about to come into season. First signs to look for are that she becomes restless and her vulva starts to swell and she bleeds. It has to be said that Shibas are incredibly fastidious and you really have to check them regularly when you are expecting their season for signs of bleeding. At about the time you are expecting your bitch to come into season it would be sensible to wipe her every 48 hours or so, with a piece of cottonwool (cotton) or white tissue. Missing the first signs of the season can mean that you miss booking your chosen sire in time, especially if he is a well-used and a popular stud dog. Failing to notice the onset of her season can cause unnecessary and unwanted chaos from the local canine population on your walks out in public. While your bitch is in season it is wise to take her by car, away from her home environment, to a secluded spot for her walks and exercise; this then effectively cuts down the trail back to your door of unwelcome canine visitors.

At the first sign of blood you should phone the stud dog owner and inform them that your bitch has started her season and make arrangements for her impending visit. A bitch's season can vary enormously. It can last three weeks, or a few days or go on for four or five weeks, which makes it very difficult when trying to assess the right time for the mating. Usually the red-coloured discharge, having appeared, will grow stronger over the first seven to eight days. It then begins to pale and, around the tenth to twelfth day, it disappears altogether. This is when the eggs have been released and it should indicate that the bitch is ready for mating. Occasionally the colour does not clear and you could find yourself waiting until her season has finished without there being any change whatsoever in colour. Watch her when she is in the garden; if your neighbour has a dog, you may well find her flirting with him through the fence. If he is going berserk and she is twitching her tail on one side at him and thrusting her rear end through the fence, you can be sure that she is ready for mating.

If you have no dogs close to you, try scratching your fingers at the base of the tail on her lower back. When she is ready she will flick her tail to one side, again indicating her readiness to mate. A hurried phone-call to the stud dog owner to say you are on your way is in order. It should be said that some bitches will stand for the male for several days, while others may only stand for one day, so pin-pointing the correct time is imperative.

If you are travelling quite a distance to the male, your vet can do a simple clinical test on your bitch to determine the right time to go. This consists of taking a vaginal swab and checking it under the microscope. The vet can determine the changes in the cell structures which, in turn, indicate when the eggs are ready to be released, thus highlighting the time for mating.

THE MATING

When mating your bitch for the first time it is important that you are with her to give her assurance, support and confidence in what, for her, is a new experience in a strange place with strange people and, moreover, with a persistent and strange male making advances to her!

Try to make the journey as calm and uneventful as possible for your Shiba. On your arrival give her time to settle after the journey and spend a penny. Perhaps let her spend a little time outside getting acclimatised to the unfamiliar surroundings. The stud dog owner normally will have everything under control and have a procedure that they follow for matings. Some stud dog owners prefer the bitch's owners not to be present at the mating, as they feel that the owners' presence will distract the female from the job in hand. Many owners are happy to let the mating be handled by the professionals. I personally am happy for the owners to stay and help where and when necessary, if that is the owners' wish. Their presence is reassurance for the bitch.

Shibas being the very basic and uncomplicated dogs that they are, perform best as nature intended. We always, initially, run the pair either side of a fence just to let them get acquainted and for the bitch to flirt with the male. After a short while we then let them run together in a confined space, well away from other dogs and away from any distractions. Sometimes, to begin with, the bitch will play hard to get, but the Shiba male is a confident alpha in all he does and he will get on with the job quickly.

101

It is important that you are close at hand to control and steady the female once the male has mounted and tied on her. A tie is when the dog mounts the bitch and penetrates her and then turns away from her, so they are then standing back-to-back but attached. With Shiba males this is usually done in a flash. I found my stud dogs always to be totally in control of the situation and in no need of assistance in attaining this end. A tie can last from a few minutes to an hour, but about ten to twenty minutes is usual. At the start of the tie your bitch may scream and shout – as only a Shiba can – but this is quite normal in all matings and she will quickly subside. Keeping the female calm and composed until the break is usually best done by her owners. The male will stay composed without any undue problems.

A slip mating is when the dog penetrates the female and ejaculates, as far as one can tell, but does not tie. In other words, he comes away from the bitch and is not attached. Puppies can still be produced from such a mating, but I personally would always suggest that a second mating take place some twenty-four hours later to be on the safe side. Puppies could be conceived at both times. Two matings are usually sufficient. Most stud dog owners will only allow the second mating to take place with a day's gap between the matings, but no later than that, thus eliminating the risk of some whelps being more advanced than others at the time of whelping.

The mating should take place in as calm and relaxed an atmosphere as possible, with only the minimum of people necessary in attendance for the dogs' needs. At the break of the tie, the bitch should be taken away to rest. Do not let her pass water for at least an hour. She should have had sufficient time to relieve herself before the mating, and you should not allow her to drink too much in the hours prior to being mated. Once she has been mated, it is a good idea to put her either into her crate, if you are at home, or into your car ready for the journey home.

At this time it is usual to pay for the stud and receive your receipt. Do remember that your Shiba may still be able to conceive for several more days, so be extra vigilant with her. Keep to the routine already mentioned until she has well finished her season and you know it is safe to take her out and about as normal.

The gestation period for most bitches is sixty-three days, though puppies can be safely born several days before or several days after that. I had a Shiba bitch that produced seven days early, totally unaided, and she produced one puppy. We had gone to the Club's AGM and came home to find mother and daughter snuggled up and feeding, all matter of fact – but this, again, is the uncomplicated Shiba. You should be organised for the whelping of your litter well in advance in preparation for just such an eventuality.

CARE DURING PREGNANCY
Once the mating has taken place, you will be anxious to know if your bitch has conceived but there will be no visible signs in the early weeks to give you any indications, for the Shiba seems to carry her puppies very high up under the rib cage. At about five or six weeks one of the first signs that she is in whelp is that

Seven days to go before whelping, and the bitch has noticeably thickened around the middle.

Photo: Lesley Wright.

Prior to whelping, the hair around the nipples will disappear, and the nipples will increase in size.

Photo: Lesley Wright.

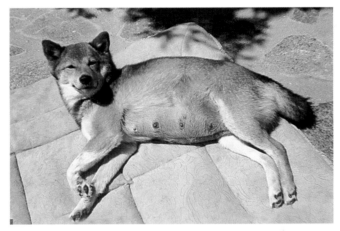

her nipples will go pink. She may quieten down a little and take a bit more care of herself, but this is not always the case with the Shiba. Some vets will do a scan of the bitch if it is really imperative that you know whether she is in whelp or not, but I would suggest that it is best not to put your Shiba through procedures that are unnecessary. Let nature takes its course and keep its secrets until 'production day'.

There is no need to change your Shiba's diet in the early weeks providing she is on a good-quality diet. There is an old saying that 'You only get out what you put in' and it is important that the diet for all your Shibas is well-balanced and nutritional throughout their lives, and especially through pregnancy.

I advocate giving a bitch in whelp Vitamin E – wheat-germ capsules daily as an addition; it helps to make whelping easier. As she progresses towards whelping the bitch's appetite may increase; it is wise then to cut down on the carbohydrates and increase the proteins, for she does not need to be carrying lots of excess weight, but only growing, healthy puppies. You may find that some days her appetite is not so good, but this is perfectly normal. Tempt her with small morsels of her favourite food just to stimulate her appetite. As the puppies develop in her and take up space, you may need to feed her more frequently, giving smaller meals to help combat this change and making it more comfortable for her.

At six or seven weeks your Shiba will be showing signs of thickening around her middle and maybe will need to relieve herself more frequently. Shibas can give birth to up to seven puppies, which is astonishing when you think of their size and the size of the puppies at birth, who can weigh anything from six to ten ounces. At around eight weeks her mammary glands may secrete fluid and will have increased in size. Occasionally your Shiba will secrete a clear discharge from her vulva; this is normal, but if the discharge is coloured then a word and a check-up with your vet is advisable.

Life for your Shiba should continue as normal throughout her pregnancy, for she is pregnant, not ill. She will still need her exercise and fun times. When the time to slow up comes, your Shiba will make the adjustments. Pampering and fussing over her will only make her more likely to play on it, for Shibas are incredibly smart!

OWNING A STUD DOG
Owning a stud dog is a great responsibility and not something that should be undertaken lightly. Serious breeders will spend a lifetime trying to improve their breed, trying to ensure that the stock they produce will conform with their idea of what is correct in conformation and temperament. For these breeders, achieving a high quality

in their stock is paramount, but it could be lost if bitches are mated to the 'dog next door'. As I have mentioned, using a dog because he is handy, he lives just down the road and his stud fee is cheap, is no basis for breeding. Those people who breed in such a way are merely reducing dog breeding to a commercial level and should not be encouraged. Owning a stud dog is not to be considered as having a money-making machine on the premises for the use of all and sundry, but a privilege, and one that you must safeguard and nurture for the betterment of the breed you love.

This is not to imply that only the well-known kennels have the superior dogs for stud – for how often have you let a puppy go to a pet home and, on seeing it some year or so later, you find it has turned out to be absolutely first-class and a superb specimen of the breed.

Having decided that you own a dog good enough to be used at stud you have to decide what his stud fees are going to be. In general it is felt that the average price of a puppy at eight weeks is a good guideline to follow – though it must be said, you may have paid a high price for perhaps the pick of litter for showing and breeding when you bought your Shiba. At the end of the day the fee may well be governed by supply and demand and, as we said at the beginning of this chapter, all too many litters are planned on the basis of convenience.

Using a well-known stud dog gives the prospective breeder the peace of mind that, firstly, he produces and, secondly, his stock will be in the ring and elsewhere. Having seen what he produces to the many different lines of bitches may help in the decision-making.

Most stud dog owners prefer the bitches to be brought to them. They are usually very busy people with many other dog commitments; they have no doubt spent many, many years building up their bloodlines and now feel that if someone wishes to take advantage of that work, then they should be expected to bring the bitch to the dog. Occasionally it is preferable to leave the bitch for a few days to be sure of getting the right day for mating; if this is your preference, then the question of housing the bitch has to be addressed and arrangements made to cover this.

As mentioned before, I prefer the owners of the female to be present when she is mated. They can then see for themselves that the mating took place and that the dog of their choice was used. The bitch will usually be more confident too if her owners are present.

A stud dog owner will have normally used his stud on several of his own bitches to determine, firstly, that he does produce and, secondly, to determine what he produces to differently bred bitches. He will have seen the resulting litters and will know how they have grown on. As the stud dog owner you will want to be able to show off your dog's progeny and claim the first honours of his success for yourself. When you have spent years promoting a particular line and having faith in your judgement, then there is no greater pleasure than seeing first-class stock that is from your breeding lines being handled and shown successfully by other people.

The whole basis of pedigree dog breeding is that man controls it. Take away that control and very quickly you will merely have dogs. You will have lost the opportunity of being able to pursue the desired traits you wish to see in a dog, such as good temperaments and the characteristics that are special to your chosen breed. You could also then find yourself in the position of someone who buys a sweet little furry mongrel who eventually grows up to be a big, unpredictable, hairy monster that attacks everything in sight.

At the other end of the spectrum is the person who owns a Shiba male who thinks that his dog must have a female. He rings up the owners of a Shiba bitch and offers them his dog's services for free, because he feels his dog should be allowed just one chance of trying 'this mating game'; or he says his dog is such a nice dog he should have a chance of being a father. What of the future of the puppies! We all think our dogs are wonderful and have much to offer, but let us be realistic and, more important, let us be responsible owners. Does this person realise that once his male has been used at stud his whole attitude could change? His dog could become more aggressive, more dominant, more territorial and this could mean the dog could start 'marking his territory' all over the house and garden, culminating in the owners thinking the dog has become 'dirty'.

Stud work can be arduous and very demanding, and it should not be taken lightly. It can be very hard on the knees, for that is where you spend most of the time during a mating. Sometimes the bitch is far from co-operative and it takes patience, understanding and experience to determine whether, in fact, she is ready to accept the male. Sometimes although a bitch is ready, she will fight tooth and nail to keep the dog from her.

Tact is also a requirement needed by a stud dog owner, for occasionally a bitch will be brought along for assessment for breeding and immediately you can see that she should not be bred from. Diplomacy is needed in persuading the owner that, though she is a wonderful pet and companion, breeding should not, in your opinion, be undertaken with her. You then will need to explain the reasons why. Though disappointed, if you have made a sound case, the owners will accept it.

There will, of course, always be the owners that will ignore your advice and take their bitch elsewhere for mating, and there will always be some unscrupulous person who will take their fee and let their dog mate the bitch. This is their prerogative, but at least you know you have been honest with them and any resulting problems cannot be attached to you and your kennel. Owning a stud dog is a great responsibility. The breed's future depends on the puppies that are produced, whether they are good, bad or indifferent.

GENETICS
Though it is possible to have a successful breeding programme over the years using just your own personal intuition as guidance in selecting the different partners and breeding lines, it will not be easy to control the outcomes to any great degree without some genetic understanding. The more you come to understand genetics, the more predictable and successful will be your breeding programme. Genetics is the study of inherent characteristics passed down the generations. Genes are the 'units of inheritance'. Combining and interchanging these genes is how you create and produce the separate distinct traits and adaptations that make up the individual animals. Every single characteristic is inherited through the genes – the genotype which is the genetic make-up, and the phenotype, which is the outward appearance. The permutations are endless. There are, however, certain dominant basic characteristics which will reproduce; the mouth is one of these.

There is a set number of chromosomes that make up each cell of the animal. The dog has 78, which are arranged in 39 pairs. The chromosomes are made up of genes. Think of the genes as beads – string them together and you have a chromosome. The pattern is different only in the germ cells, which are the reproductive cells. In the germ cells there is only half the number of chromosomes present. The male's sperm carries the reproduction chromosomes and the female's egg carries her chromosomes. When mating has taken place, the sperm penetrates the egg and the two combine to bring the number of chromosomes up to the level that is required for that species, and thus a new life-form is developed.

The chromosomes which determine the sex of the offspring can be identified in the male as the pair that has the X and the Y chromosome together. In the female the sex-determining pair of chromosomes will be the two X chromosomes together. Putting these chromosomes together from the parents in the different permutations will determine the sexes of each puppy, while the combining of the genes contained in them will pass on the various characteristics that will be exclusive to that puppy.

All the puppies from a particular mating will have a similar genetic background but, depending which genes they have inherited from the different parent, their characteristics will be individual to them. Line-breeding strengthens a particular characteristic provided that both parents have that characteristic. While this characteristic may be visible, sometimes the characteristic can lie 'dormant'; this is called 'a recessive'. Though an ancestor may have had the characteristic, it has not surfaced in this animal, but he will still carry the gene.

Genetics is a very complex subject. I have tried just to highlight some of its finer points. The more you are able to read on the subject and the more you are able to absorb can only, long-term, be of benefit to you and to our Shibas.

9 *WHELPING*

Being well prepared for your forthcoming litter is crucial, and it can be a costly exercise, but the expenditure can be offset against future litters. If you have the right facilities and the right equipment these can last you for many years to come. If you are going to breed with your Shibas, then you owe it to them to give them the best you can afford, or you should not be breeding, for this is an undertaking that you have embarked upon, it is not your Shiba's decision. There is one fundamental piece of equipment and that is the whelping box. This is the first home the puppies will know, and it is where your Shiba bitch is going to spend at least the first two weeks after whelping, while she is rearing the puppies.

THE WHELPING BOX

Ten to fourteen days before your Shiba is due to whelp you should have prepared a whelping box. This is a box usually made of wood or plastic. Your Shiba needs to be able to lie stretched out in it, but it does not need to be so big that the puppies can crawl away to a corner and then not be able to get back to mum. The measurements should be about three foot wide by four foot long, with three high sides of about eighteen inches. The fourth side should be left open, with just a low parapet, about three inches high, to keep out draughts and to allow the bitch to be able to step over it when she is getting in and out. It does not need to have a top or roof on it.

You will need a guard-rail, about three inches high and four-sided, that can be placed in the whelping box a few inches away from the sides. This is for the puppies' protection and gives them space to escape from the mother as she lies herself down. Though they are wonderful mothers, the Shiba bitch is not known for her tact, and is quite prone to jumping into the box and sitting where she lands, usually sending pups scattering in all directions, or lying down with a puppy trapped behind her. Though the whelp will scream in protest, there may not always be someone at hand to hear and thus prevent a tragedy. This rail is only to be used once the puppies have arrived and until they are large and strong enough to be able to escape from their mother's entrances. As the puppies grow, I extend the box with a run – but more of that later.

It is well worth visiting a dog show prior to your litter's arrival, for you will see several types of whelping boxes on sale, plus literature on different types. If you are going to be having more litters it is well worth purchasing a professionally made whelping box; it will last you for years. If you decide to make your own, looking at whelping boxes will also give you ideas about how it is done and what design best suits your needs.

The whelping box should be easy to wash or scrub. I always use vet-bed in the base of mine. I find it is warm and it gives traction for when the puppies are moving around, it saves them from slipping and it is easy for washing. However, while I am actually whelping the bitch I only use paper for the base of the box – I have a roll of white wall-lining paper which is easy to tear off as I need it – although I know many breeders use newspaper all the time with a litter of puppies.

The whelping box should be placed in a room that is reasonably quiet and is not being constantly used by the family – spare bedroom or study perhaps, but it does need to be on the ground floor with easy access to the garden. If you are fortunate enough to have a whelping room it should still be adjacent to the house because of the socialising and human contact which will be needed by the puppies from the earliest weeks of their life. The room needs to be warm and well ventilated. Ours has a glass door for observation, which allows us to monitor without having to enter and disturb mother and babies when they have arrived.

A comfortable chair in the whelping room is a must, for you will be spending many hours, at the whelping and after, just watching the mother and her babies develop. Puppies are great time wasters!

HEATING

Though many breeds seem to need an infra-red lamp over the box, I have found that the Shiba seems unhappy with this, so I maintain a good warmth throughout the room rather than just over the box. It is important that in the first two or three weeks the puppies are kept warm. They should be maintained at 70 degrees Fahrenheit. Puppies cannot retain body heat of their own until they are about three weeks old. I use vet-bed and heating pads to maintain their body temperature and thus keep them warm. The puppies will snuggle up to the mother for warmth and comfort, and to each other when mother leaves the box to relieve herself and to eat. If the bitch gets too hot and is uncomfortable she will pant and the puppies will move away to cool down. With mother's constant licking and cleaning, they become damp, but they must not be allowed to become chilled.

ESSENTIAL EQUIPMENT

It is advisable to have the following items ready in the whelping room so that, should you be caught short and the bitch starts to deliver early, you have everything to hand.

● A baby alarm for fitting in the whelping room and another mobile one for moving from the kitchen during the day to your bedroom at night as the whelping becomes imminent.

• A household thermometer for checking room temperature and the area in the whelping box.

• A clinical thermometer for taking the bitch's temperature.

• Small, sterilised, blunt-ended scissors for cutting the umbilical cords.

• White cotton or thread for tying the umbilical cords before cutting them.

• Plenty of towels for drying the puppies as they are born.

• A bowl, a supply of water, disinfectant and a nail scrubbing brush for washing your hands.

• A clock, in order to observe the intervals between whelpings.

• A cardboard box, low-sided, about two-foot square, in which you place the puppies which have already been born, as the mother gives birth to the next whelp.

• A hot-water bottle and a towel to cover it, which is placed in the bottom of the cardboard box

• A roll of white wall lining paper for the base of the box during whelping.

• Kitchen scales for weighing the puppies.

• A notebook and pencil for recording information.

• If numerous puppies are born, I use different-coloured knitting wool to identify them, which I tie loosely around their necks. It is important to change this frequently as the puppy grows, so that it does not become too tight.

• A water dish for the bitch and glucose to add to the water as a supplement for her throughout the whelping.

• For emergencies I always have a premature baby feeder handy just in case one of the puppies should have problems suckling.

• A milk substitute or lactol just in case you need to hand-feed one of the puppies.

APPROACHING WHELPING
If this is your first whelping you may feel happier having an experienced breeder along for support. You should make arrangements well in advance with someone and, as the time draws near, keep daily contact with them. Keep this book handy in the whelping room just in case you get caught short and find yourself whelping in the middle of the night on your own. Shibas are notorious for producing nocturnally. However, as I have said before, they are wonderful mothers and even the maiden bitch has complete confidence in her own abilities and just seems to get on with the job in hand. They rarely need your assistance – only your reassurance and your calming influence.

About a week to ten days before the bitch is due to whelp, introduce her to the whelping room and whelping box. I enclose the Shiba in there when I go out, and at night, so that she becomes familiar with it and is happy and comfortable in there.

The sign that the whelping is imminent is the loss of hair around her nipples. This is nature's way of clearing a way for the puppies to find the nipples unhampered. If the hair does not clear it is wise to trim carefully around the nipple area. The nipples become dark pink and, of course, will have enlarged.

The bitch's appetite may wane in the last week or two, but it is important for the growing puppies that whatever food she does take in is very nutritional; so tempt her with meat, chicken, liver and milk. In the last two weeks the puppies do the most growing in the womb of the mother, so small but frequent meals are necessary. I make sure that throughout the last two weeks I am at home and, if I need to go out, that it is only for short periods at a time. I try also to leave someone in the house just in case, with a phone number telling them where to contact me.

It is important to keep a wary eye on your Shiba. You will notice her shape will change as the puppies move down from her rib-cage and fill out her waist. She will, hopefully, calm down and not be so exuberant – though this is not always the case with the Shiba. Shortly before a bitch is due to whelp her temperature will drop to below 100 degrees F (38 degrees C) about twelve hours before whelping. The temperature is taken by inserting the thermometer into the rectum and you should start taking her temperature from around the fifty-seventh day. If you are not happy taking her temperature, then there are other signs to look for.

Several days before whelping she will start to nest; this means that she will scratch at the paper in her whelping box and shred it and fluff it up for a nest. She will go off her food, usually a day before whelping, and refuse to eat anything; sometimes she will vomit, though this should not be excessive. She will be restless and seem unable to settle comfortably. It is important that you are aware of the changes in her. When she goes out in the garden to relieve herself she must be accompanied, for I have known a puppy to be born during just one of these excursions.

Several days before the whelping is due we switch the baby alarm on at night in the whelping room and in our bedroom so that, at the slightest sound or disturbance in the whelping box, we are aware of it and can go and investigate. Some breeders set up a bed in the whelping room in order to be on hand during the event and for several nights after the puppies are born.

THE WHELPING
As the time gets nearer for your Shiba to whelp, her nesting efforts become more in earnest and she will become reluctant to leave the box. Initially, she will be turning round and licking and cleaning her vulva. Her waters will have broken, which is why she is cleaning herself, and a clear, white, mucous discharge will have been produced from her vulva, which signals that the seal on the womb has been broken and the puppies are on their way. The vulva will have softened. She will start to pant, and labour will begin. It is wise to give your vet a call to let him know that this stage has been reached so that, should you need him, he will be on hand.

We would never knowingly leave a bitch to whelp on her own, for she or the puppies may need your help and, no matter how many litters you have seen born, the miracle of birth is still a wonder to behold that never ceases to amaze.

Make a note of the time that the bitch began labour. Shibas have a very low pain tolerance and, as labour begins in earnest, the bitch will stand, sit and move around, indicating that the puppies are on the move down the birth channel and she is feeling uncomfortable. You

The litter 24 hours after birth.   *Photo: Lesley Wright.*

will notice her contractions becoming stronger and more frequent as a puppy is imminent. She will, of course, if she is a maiden bitch, be bewildered and shocked as the first whelp emerges and that is where your reassurance and presence is so important to her.

Shibas seem to make very little fuss about giving birth – a few pants and a few strains and, usually, a very big scream and there is the first puppy delivered. Try to sit back and observe; let the bitch get on with her duties; try not to interfere unless it is absolutely necessary.

Each puppy will usually make its entrance into the world inside a sac or membrane bag. The mother should remove the bag immediately, thereby allowing the puppy to start breathing, and she should begin licking and cleaning the puppy. If she delays in removing the bag and becomes preoccupied with her rear end, which is quite often the case, then you must quickly do this for her or the puppy will die. You need to break the bag away from the puppy with your fingers. You will find the puppy is attached to a placenta by a cord that is attached to its belly. The mother should sever the umbilical cord with her teeth and start to clean and dry the whelp but, again, if she does not attend to this, then you will need to deal with the cord yourself.

You will need to tie the white cotton or yarn tight around the umbilical cord, close to the puppy's abdomen, and then cut the cord about an inch away, between the thread and the placenta, severing it from the afterbirth. Do not take the puppy away from the mother while you are attending to this, but handle it there, in the box, at her side, as the removal of the puppy from the box will only agitate and upset her – and remember, this is her pride and joy and her great achievement. Your assistance must be given where she can see what is going on; for, at the end of the day, her wellbeing and peace of mind, and that of the puppy, is the all-important factor. Once you have dealt with the puppy, quickly place it back onto the mother and let it suckle. She will then attend to it and will relax until the next contractions begin.

It is important to check there is a placenta with the birth of each puppy. Quite often the mother, once she has detached the puppy from its afterbirth, will quickly eat the placenta as it is full of nutrition; but it is preferable that the bitch only eats a couple, for they also have a laxative effect.

Often, if it is the first litter for the bitch, at the birth of the first puppy she may appear confused and surprised. It may be that she thinks she has done something wrong, so be reassuring and comforting, and calm her as best you can. Sometimes the bitch will sit back and stare at the object which has suddenly appeared. If this happens, attend to the puppy first, but at the same time praise the mother and tell her how clever she is. Show her the puppy and let her lick it while still telling her how clever she is. It is a good stimulus for the puppy when the mother licks him.

The puppy needs to be dried and kept warm. If the mother is not attempting to attend to the puppy when he is first born, then you will need to assist her and show her the way. Hold him with his head down as you are drying him. Give him a vigorous towelling all over, paying special attention to the areas around his nose and mouth; remove any excess mucus that may be draining from there. The puppy may object and cry but at least then you know he is alive and breathing, and his squeals mean his lungs are fully functioning.

If the whelping-box paper becomes soiled I cover it with another sheet of paper without disturbing the mother and without making any undue fuss. I find that Shibas seem to have very little fluid debris while whelping, in contrast to other breeds.

Bitches vary in the time-span between producing their puppies. It may be that just a few minutes after producing one puppy she starts to get restless. She may stand up and start scratching at the bedding. Be careful to see that the just-produced puppy does not get trampled on or lost in her nesting antics. Once she settles herself down again, put the puppy back onto her nipple. It is imperative that each puppy suckles and takes in the colostrum, which is in the first milk released by the bitch, for this helps the puppy's own body-functions to start working.

Also, the puppy's suckling will help to stimulate the mother's contractions and thus set in motion the next whelp's arrival. She may produce her puppies in pairs, or space them out at intervals, with the first couple coming fairly quickly then, after that, half an hour or even hour may pass before any more make their entrance. I have found the Shiba, in general, to be very laid back in her approach to whelping. She seems to take every stage of whelping in a totally relaxed way, handling each stage at her own pace and in her own good time, thus giving each whelp a comforting and secure introduction to life.

As long as the bitch is relaxed and comfortable in the interim period between whelpings there is no need for alarm. She may even be relaxed enough to sleep. Should the Shiba go for a couple of hours and not produce any more puppies she may well have finished labour. Offer her a drink as she may be thirsty after her labours and a bowl of milk with some glucose added will just give her a supplementary boost. Or she may refuse anything at this stage; that is quite normal. Once the Shiba has finished whelping she will check out the arrivals and then settle down and sleep. Check that all the puppies are suckling or are nestling on her or are close to her.

While I am whelping my bitch I try to find time to check each puppy over for cleft palates or any other abnormalities. I weigh them and keep a note of the time each whelp is born. It is surprising how similar all puppies seem to be at birth, and regardless of their eventual size, there is very little difference between, say, a Boxer, a Rottweiler or Shiba Inu. Shibas are born a murky browny-grey colour. This is called their camouflage colour. It afforded them protection from predators and any other unwelcome attentions, thus giving them a chance of survival in the early days of their existence when they were born on the mountainsides open to the elements.

PROBLEM BIRTHS

If she is still restless and seems agitated, or if she is straining but nothing is forthcoming, it may be that the bitch has a problem whelp. It may be a large puppy that she is having difficulty passing, or the puppy may be caught across the birth channel or it may be a breech birth, where the puppy comes feet-first instead of the normal head-first, so any remaining puppies are then held up in the birth process until the offending whelp has been born.

This situation should not be allowed to last longer than ten to fifteen minutes. Have a word with your vet. He may well come out and check her. However, if he asks you to take her to his surgery, be calm and reassuring while preparing the mother and her babies for the journey. Do not separate the mother from the puppies, as this will only cause her more anxieties. Taking the puppies along will give the vet an opportunity to check the whelps. When there is a problem it is better to take the bitch to the surgery, for the vet has all his equipment to hand should the need arise, plus the assistance of his nurses.

The vet may suggest you give the mother the opportunity to go outside into the garden to relieve herself. Be sure, if you do this, to watch carefully, in case she produces a bundle outside. If your vet comes out to the bitch, he will probably give her a pituitrin injection which will stimulate her contractions and, if any puppies remain, it will start them on their way down the birth canal. It will also clear out any afterbirths that she may have retained. It may be that your bitch has become fatigued by the births and this injection just stimulates the womb to get on with and finish the job in hand.

INERTIA

A condition that can occur with a bitch in whelp is inertia. This can occur in the first or second stages of labour. It means that the bitch has an inability to produce her whelps. Primary inertia can preclude her from going into whelp at all. This can happen because she is going to produce a small litter, so the hormones required to get the contractions started are not produced in sufficient amounts. Secondary inertia will sometimes occur after the bitch has produced a large litter. The uterus becomes over-stretched and the bitch becomes tired; the uterus then stops contracting. Your vet will usually give a pituitrin injection to try to get the uterus to resume contractions. Sometimes taking the bitch outside and walking her round can get her started. I have even heard that popping her into the back of a car and taking her on a bumpy ride can have the desired effect, although I would have thought this would be more effective if the bitch was overdue and just needed a jolt to get things going. Be guided by your vet who may, after having tried all other procedures, decide to do a caesarean section.

CAESAREAN SECTIONS

Occasionally a bitch will experience a problem with the birth of a puppy and if all else fails your vet may have to do a caesarean section on her. This means he has to operate and deliver the puppy through the stomach wall. I have only experienced this with my other breeds, never with a Shiba. Also, in my experience, it has always been a success and has saved the unborn puppy or puppies from an unnecessary demise.

Once a caesarean has been performed and the puppies delivered you will be able to take the bitch and the puppies home. She will usually be fully awake by the time you arrive home. Do not put the puppies onto the bitch until she is fully *compos mentis*. If she has produced some of the puppies prior to the operation, then re-introduce them to her one at a time and she should readily accept them. If she has had a caesarean to deliver all the puppies, then she is going to be confused and puzzled by their appearance, so you must introduce them gradually, reassuring her and praising her for her competence. She should not be left until you are one hundred per cent happy that she has accepted her whelps and is paying attention to their needs.

It is imperative that all the puppies should have suckled and taken in their share of the colostrum antibodies that her milk produces in the first twenty-four to forty-eight hours after whelping. Special care needs to be taken of her after a caesarean so that her stitches do not pop. Stitches are sometimes of the dissolving kind and therefore they do not need taking out and some have to be removed after a week or so, but your vet will tell you about this. Your bitch will very quickly get over this procedure and its amazing how quickly they resume their normal parental duties as if the whelping was normal.

It is important to discuss with your vet the reasons for your bitch's inability to whelp without the help of the operation, for this must be taken into account if you wish to breed from her again in the future. It may well be that she should not be bred from again.

RESUSCITATING PUPPIES

Stillborn puppies will occasionally occur because they have spent too long in the birth canal. If you are confident that the puppy otherwise looks normal, it may have just expired from lack of oxygen. Resuscitation can be tried quickly. You should discreetly take the puppy away from the bitch by occupying her with one of the healthy whelps. Rub the puppy briskly by using the towel on its back and on its chest, having first cleared its air-ways around its nose and mouth. There is usually a quick response. However, failing this, cradle the puppy in both hands. Support his head and neck with one hand. With the other hand support his body. Hold him so that he is lying on his back, with his head down and with his tongue forward, and swing him up and down between your legs.

Failing this, a sniff of smelling salts, or a spot of neat brandy on his tongue can produce the gasps for breath you want him to take, and thus get him breathing. If the puppy has been dead a long time his tongue will be white and it is then best to let him rest in peace.

RETAINED PLACENTAS

This is when the bitch has not expelled all the afterbirths or placentas. If you have any doubts, it is usual for the vet to give an injection at the end of whelping to cover this eventuality. A retained placenta can set up an infection in the bitch which affects her milk and then, in turn, the puppies.

10 CARING FOR THE LITTER

When the whelping is over you will find that your bitch is reluctant to leave her puppies even to go out and relieve herself. This is quite normal. When you can persuade her to go out, accompany her into the garden and keep a sharp eye on her, just in case she produces any more pups, for sometimes there may be another one lurking up under her ribcage that even the most discerning of eyes has missed. She will want to return to her charges as soon as possible. The paper in the box will need changing – I usually get my husband to attend to this while I am in the garden with the mother.

It is at this stage that we change the paper for the vet-bed and place the guard-rail in the whelping box for the protection of the puppies. The Shiba mother is very nimble on her feet and manages to avoid the puppies most of the time when she jumps back into the box. She also seems to be much more concerned and careful when settling herself back down into the box with her puppies, turning round and round until she finds a space that she can safely lie

down in. It is not so with all breeds, for we have many a time, when whelping other breeds, said "If they survive their mother and her clumsiness, they will survive anything!"

If possible, I like to sponge her rear end just to freshen her up before she returns to her puppies and the clean whelping box; but if she is unhappy with this then leave it till the next day.

The Shiba mother is happy to be left to nurse her whelps, so a well-earned break for the helper is appreciated. Leave the room quietly so as not to disturb the mother. On your return, mother and babies should be quiet and content and it should be a scene of serene tranquillity. The bitch will be glad to be taking a rest. Observation should indicate that the puppies are sucking strongly. They seem to knead their mother with their front paws while suckling at the same time. This kneading, in fact, is stimulating the milk flow through the nipples and into their mouths. Their coats should all be dried out and looking velvety and they should already be looking a little rounder and not as long and lean as they do at

117

birth. The vet will normally call the following day to check the mother to see that her womb has contracted and that there is no bad discharge. He may also give an injection of antibiotic to ward off any infection. He will also check the puppies over, making sure none are showing any signs of dehydration, which would indicate that they are not feeding.

MONITORING THE LITTER

The temperature in the whelping box should be maintained at around 70 degrees Fahrenheit; remember that the puppies are unable to generate their own body heat for several weeks. Keep a watchful eye on the puppies. Occasionally one will crawl away from the mother and the rest of the litter and find himself in a corner. The bitch will not wish to disturb the remaining litter if they are suckling just to fetch him back to her side. It is important, therefore, that you rescue him and put him back alongside the bitch and the other puppies for warmth and food. Puppies must be feeding frequently in order to maintain themselves.

A watchful eye on mother and litter is usually all that is necessary over the next few days in respect of nursing. Your bitch may well be reluctant to eat and drink, not wishing to leave her puppies. To be sure the mother is having some sustenance I mix a raw egg-yolk (not the white) into warm milk to which I have also added a measure of liquid calcium. Alternatively, some water with glucose added can also be offered to her. Never leave dishes of liquid in the box, just in case any puppies find their way into it and drown. In the first few days the puppies will spend all the time suckling and sleeping. Mother will take care of all their needs, frequently topping and tailing them. This is not always to their liking but she knows what has to be done and she gets on and does it. She will lick and clean the remains of the umbilical cord until, within a few days, it dries up and falls off.

HANDLING THE PUPPIES

I handle the puppies from day one, under the watchful eye of the mother, even though I may only be placing them on her teats. This is necessary for many reasons but, most important, I feel that they must have human contact right from the start, and the mother must accept my assistance for the benefit of all concerned. Again, the Shiba mother does not usually have any problems with this. Any handling of the puppies must be done in the whelping box and with mother in full view. Even if you are weighing the puppies, this must be done in the box.

The puppies should be handled gently, calmly and carefully; any sudden jolts or quick movements may scare them and they will scream. This, in turn, will upset and unnerve the mother, so caution and care are necessary. The mother will quickly accept your help, and it will be a matter of course to her that you are both involved together with these puppies.

THE AILING PUPPY

A thriving puppy is a contented puppy; having eaten he then sleeps. Should you have a puppy that is crying or wailing, it may be that he has a problem feeding. Check him out. Does he have a problem getting on a nipple and staying there? Is he being pushed aside by his stronger brothers and sisters? If so, each time you go to look at the litter, make sure you put him on the nipple. With your thumb and index finger pinch up the skin on the back of his neck. Does it return quickly to the neck area or does it pull down slowly, puckering slightly? This is a good way to test whether or not the pup is dehydrated. Puppies can weaken very quickly, so if in doubt, have your vet look at him.

Occasionally a bitch will push a puppy away to one side as if discarding it, and this is often what is actually happening. Check the puppy out for any visible signs that may be untoward. Have your vet look at him. The mother usually does this if there is something wrong.

CARING FOR THE MOTHER
While the diet throughout the mother's pregnancy has been important, now that she has puppies to feed it becomes even more important that she is having a high-protein diet and plenty of water in order to produce plenty of milk for them.

You usually have to coax mothers to resume eating, but in a breed like the Shiba, which is totally unmotivated by food at the best of times, this can be even more difficult. Cooked chicken or fish are the safest bet and if they have to be hand-fed to her, then that is what you do. Little and often is the secret Add natural calcium to her diet as a supplement. Water in a bowl outside of the box should always be readily available.

Thankfully, Shiba mothers very quickly get over the novelty of puppies and will be happy to skip out of the whelping box to see what else is happening in the world outside. I leave the bitch a square of vet-bed to rest on outside of the box – but do not make it too comfortable, for she may prefer to stay there and not tend her puppies in the box.

The mother's wellbeing is of the utmost importance and she should be checked daily. The discharge from her vulva post-whelping and for a couple of days will be unbecoming and dark. The colour will then change to a blood-red and this will eventually fade off completely. The discharge is caused by bleeding from the surface of the uterus where the placentas have detached themselves. The discharge should not remain thick and dark for more than a few days; if it does, have a word with your vet without delay. Any unpleasant odour should also be checked out.

Check that the bitch's nipples are not sore or lumpy and also examine the surrounding area of the nipple; sometimes this becomes sore from the puppies' constant kneading. There should be no swelling or hardness around the teat areas that could lead to milk fever or mastitis. You will have to examine these areas frequently. As the puppies grow, their nails will have to be trimmed regularly, to minimise scratching the mother.

The growth of the puppies in the early weeks is phenomenal – they seem to grow before your eyes. They take an enormous amount out of the bitch and she should be monitored daily for signs of distress or fatigue that could be an indication of something more serious, like eclampsia or mastitis (see the chapter on ailments). If you are unsure, always have your vet check the mother.

It is important that the bitch's diet is

also closely monitored and that it is increased as she requires, for the health, growth and well-being of the puppies depends on the mother, and without her, your task of rearing would be increased a hundredfold and still not be as good as the mother's.

When the bitch is taken out to relieve herself, it must be in an area that is not frequented by any other dogs, for it is imperative that she does not transmit any germs back to the nest and her puppies. It is best to keep a section of your garden just for her use until the puppies are weaned. The Shiba mother's motions will be loose to begin with. This is due perhaps in part to her having devoured too many placentas but mainly to her constant cleaning and relieving the puppies of their faeces.

THE FIRST TWO WEEKS

At the end of the first week the puppies will have doubled in size. They will be moving around the whelping box. Their bodies will be rounding and filling out and their coats will be looking plusher,

their ears will be up but not yet open. The umbilical cords in the main will have dried up and fallen off, leaving a nice clean belly button. For the first two weeks the puppies are totally dependent on the mother to provide constant care, feeding and stimulus-cleaning them, thus relieving them of their of faeces. They will sleep 90 per cent of the time.

By the end of the second week their eyes will have begun to open. Shibas do seem to be slower then many other breeds in this respect, but having said that, it certainly has no bearing on the rate at which they are, by then, moving around the whelping box. They are like furry slugs. The heads are taking shape, and once their eyes open their adorable facial expressions become apparent.

Gentle handling of each and every puppy is a must throughout the early weeks. It should become the norm. At the beginning the puppies shrug and resent it and will turn their heads from yours if you kiss them, but daily handling and fondling soon becomes a pleasure to them. The human contact

The mother should appear relaxed and contented, and all the puppies should be feeding.

Photo: Kirsten Jorgensen.

At just over two weeks old the puppies become more aware of each other.

Photo: Kirsten Jorgensen.

aspect is paramount to the Shiba's development from the very first days of life. While the Shiba mother is out in the exercise area or having her meal I will sit in the whelping box with the puppies, so that they get use to the smell of me and accept me.

THE LITTER AT THREE WEEKS
At three weeks the fat chubby heads are only surpassed by their fat chubby bodies. The colour of the coat should begin to clear and should be giving some indication of the colour they are finally going to be. But, as many of us know, this is not a certainty. As registrations at the Kennel Club will bear out, many colour descriptions on the document-ation of registration bear no resemblance to the colour that the Shiba attains in later life. The puppies become aware of their litter mates and will nuzzle each other. Sitting is done with ease, standing is a little more precarious. While the front legs seem to know what to do, the back legs seem to find it a little more difficult. A litter of puppies is a

notorious time-waster, for I spend hours just sitting and watching them develop, watching their different characters and antics. They are all-absorbing and a wonder to behold. It is a fact that no matter how many litters you have, you never outgrow or tire of the pleasure they give you.

The reason that I always whelp my litters in the house is so that I can constantly observe them. The normal household noises like the washing-machine, the vacuum cleaner, doors opening and closing are something the puppies become familiar with and accept as part of the normal run of things. With dogs, it is always very apparent which ones have been whelped and reared in kennels, and which have spent their early days in the house, because of how their attitudes differ.

The Shiba mother is quite happy to leave the puppies for periods of time by this stage, and then go back into the whelping box to feed and clean the puppies. I leave a bed outside the box so that she can rest away from the litter

THE LITTER AT THREE WEEKS
Photos: John Daniels.

ABOVE: The five puppies assembled – with difficulty!

BELOW: The puppies gain confidence from each other.

Even at this early stage, the male (left) is easily distinguished from his sister.

ABOVE: The puppies are mobile, but progress is still tentative.

RIGHT: Concentrations spans are very small, but the puppy should appear alert and interested in what is going on.

In the first few weeks, the majority of the time is still divided between eating and sleeping, with occasional intervals of play.

when she feels the need to. If there are several puppies in the litter, their combined sizes usually dwarf the mother and she is glad to have some respite from them.

THE LITTER AT FOUR WEEKS
At four weeks the puppies are aware of noises and follow you with their eyes. Moving around on all four legs has become a cinch. Rough-and-tumble with each other becomes fun. The puppies will be moving away from their bedded area to relieve themselves. An extension to the whelping box is now necessary. It should still retain the puppies but be low enough for mother to access it. The extension should be papered, although the sleeping area remains covered with vet-bed.

This is also the start of their toilet training. Shibas are undoubtedly one of the cleanest and most fastidious breeds you will ever come across – perhaps only equalled by their big cousin, the Akita. The breed will only foul as far away from their sleeping quarters as is possible, so they must be given the space to do this. Pack order within the litter now becomes apparent, as do their sexual explorations.

If the weather is good and dry I like to allow the puppies time out in the garden. It should be in an enclosed area that no other dogs have been allowed on. A puppy pen is a must for these excursions and also for later use. It should be about six foot by four foot in size and placed on a concrete base; a garden terrace is fine. Put a square of bedding in a corner for the puppies to lie on. At the first excursion they will be apprehensive and unsure, but if initially you sit in there with them, they will quickly settle and then explore as they become used to the pen. Be sure to keep a watchful eye on the puppies: they should not be allowed to get cold, wet or dirty.

WEANING

I am never in a hurry to wean Shibas, for I feel that, provided the mother is happy to feed the puppies and has plenty of milk to do so, then they are getting the best start in life and receiving the immunity they need. I start to wean at around four to five weeks of age, although I will start earlier if I think it is in the best interest of the mother.

At first, I take the bitch away from the pups for a couple of hours a day, usually in the morning, after she has spent the night with them. Mother is glad to go outside in the garden, to have her breakfast and to romp. It is good for her to have time to herself and relax. It also gives me time to groom her and spend some time checking her over. When she is away from the puppies she should be sufficiently out of earshot of the puppies and their romping. If the mother hears yelping or crying from the puppies she will want to return to them immediately. The time she spends away from the puppies should become longer and longer through the day.

Begin by introducing a little baby cereal with evaporated milk slightly watered down, or goat's milk if you are fortunate enough to be able to get it. The consistency should be of pouring-cream. The milk should be body temperature. Also add a spot of honey. I introduce this first meal around lunch time.

It is important to decide which milk you are going to use and stick with it as changing from one to another is detrimental to the puppies. Goat's milk can be frozen, and is available from health food stores. To begin with I feed them individually from a saucer until they are able to lap. If you hold the saucer at chin level just in front of him, the puppy quickly gets the message. Once all the puppies are lapping I use a puppy feeder. This is a dish shaped like a shallow bell. This then ensures that all the puppies get around the feeder without any problem.

The second meal, a milky one, I introduce in the late evening, a couple of hours before letting the mother back in with them for the night. Any new foods should be introduced gradually over a three to four-day period. The puppies' meals should be increased to four a day by the end of six weeks – that is two milky meals and two meat or chicken meals.

Introducing meat to the diet should be done as follows. Begin with raw scraped beef. Take a piece of lean raw beef and a teaspoon. Scrape the teaspoon down the grain of the meat, leaving behind the stringy bits. The scraped meat is delicate and easily digestible and is usually accepted readily by the puppies. If you decide to wean onto one of the proprietary puppy foods, use one of the well-known makes and stick rigidly to the manufacturer's instructions. It is still important to alternate the meals with a certain amount of fresh meat, eggs and milk dishes. Shibas especially enjoy cooked chicken and also rice. If you wish to introduce this into their diet early it can be liquidised. To one of the milk feeds add the yolk of an egg, one egg yolk for every three puppies. *Do not feed the white of the egg.*

I put a bowl of water down for the puppies at regular intervals, but I do not leave it down, as the pups are apt to wade in and out of it and can end up wet and cold, apart from the mess it makes.

You will find mother is quite happy to go into the puppies and continue nursing them throughout the weaning weeks. She will lie with them initially, then, as they get bigger and rougher, she will stand for them to suckle, thus gradually drying up her milk supply. I leave the mother with the puppies at night until they are about six weeks old, but if she is reluctant to go in with them for that long then I let her call the tune.

EARLY SOCIALISATION
Once the puppies are weaned the mother will still want to visit and check on things, but once the puppies try to feed from her, she will quickly disappear from the pen. The puppies can, provided the weather is dry and fine, spend more time outside in a play pen. Sunlight is excellent for growing puppies and they seem to thrive once they are able to get outside. By this stage cleaning up after a litter of boisterous puppies can be a mammoth task, so being outside makes this easier. The run or penned area must be cleaned down daily. If it can be

attached to a kennel or shed, then by putting them inside to sleep, you are given the opportunity to clean up without the puppies assisting you.

Many pleasant and absorbing hours are spent with the puppies, socialising and playing with them when they are outside. There is nothing more rewarding than their moments with you and having the puppies clambering to get on your lap for attention. Brushing and grooming their coats at this early age gets them used to this necessary chore. Gently standing them and handling them all over, examining their mouths and teeth, also becomes something they accept as normal procedure. Family members are encouraged to spend time with the puppies from early on, just talking to them and petting them. If then I have to be away through a day, the puppies have no problem accepting their food and exercise periods with somebody else. This also becomes good grounding for when they move on to their new homes and new families. Talking to the puppies, encouraging them to explore and to accept different situations and

THE LITTER AT SIX WEEKS
Photos: John Daniels.

The puppies are fully weaned and feeding with enthusiasm.

RIGHT: The puppies establish their own pecking order within the litter.

BELOW: The mother teaches social behaviour, and the puppies learn to submit to a more dominant animal.

BOTTOM: perhaps most important of all, the puppies learn to be handled by people.

The product of excellent rearing, this puppy is ready to face the outside world.

family members, and checking them when they are being too boisterous either with a litter-mate or with me, is all part of their education. Teaching them what is acceptable and what is not is all part of the responsibility you took on when you decided to produce a litter of puppies, for the onus is on the breeder of the litter, at the end of the day, to produce a sound, stable temperament in all the puppies.

WORMING
The puppies will needing worming at least once before going to their new homes. Take your vet's advice as to when and how often. Be sure that when the new owners collect their puppy, you have the name of the worming product that you have used and details of how many times the puppy has been wormed and what, if any, injections the pup has had. This then makes it easy for the new owner's vet to continue the good practices you have initiated on behalf of the puppy.

Never worm a sick puppy; a few worms will do less harm than administering a medicine which is, after all, a poison to worms. You should never worm a puppy when you are introducing new foods to the puppy. Its digestion can only cope with so much at a time. Most puppies have worms to some degree, and the worst that can happen is that the worms deprive the puppy of some of its food. You can easily eradicate the worms in a day or so, when the time is right and the medication can be given.

VIEWING THE PUPPIES
As the puppies grow on they should be introduced to as much of life as is

possible without taking them off your home property. Over the weeks they will have had numerous visitors and prospective new owners. While we are happy for people to come and see the puppies, we are always very concerned that they do not come into close contact with the puppies initially, but that they just view them from a distance.

It is understandable that a prospective new owner will want to see his or her puppy's development in the early weeks. We usually allow viewing from four weeks and again at six weeks. We find most responsible people will respect our concern for our puppies and understand that, until the pups have had a precautionary injection, handling is out of bounds. The spreading of diseases is all too easy. We would not allow anyone that had just been to a dog show to come and see our puppies, or someone who had been in contact with other dogs. We have a disinfectant tray at the front of our home for visitors to tread through, thus disinfecting their shoes before they enter our house.

PROBLEMS IN PUPPIES
Continuous crying in a puppy is usually symptomatic of him not suckling and getting milk. Check his palate by placing a finger into the roof of his mouth. Occasionally a puppy can have what is called a cleft palate. This is where the roof of the mouth is missing so, when the puppy suckles the milk, it not only passes down the throat but it can come back down the nose, causing choking. It can also go down into the lungs. Sadly the death of the puppy quickly follows.

If a puppy is not feeding, hold him on the mother's nipple, making sure he is sucking. Every time you check on the mother, place this puppy on to her; he should be placed on her every two hours. If you feel he is still not making progress you will have to supplement him by hand-feeding. If a puppy is not feeding sufficiently he will weaken very quickly, so you must be constantly aware of the crying pup, especially if all the others are quiet and content.

If the whole litter are crying more than normal and appear bloated, check their motions. Are they greenish-coloured and is there diarrhoea? Are their anuses red and swollen? Ask your vet to come out and check them; it could be that the bitch's milk is toxic and you may have to hand-rear the puppies.

Sometimes the puppies will cry because they need to pass urine. Is the mother stimulating them to do this? If she is not, then you will have to do this for her. Using a damp swab of cotton wool, gentle rub the tummy and anus of each puppy and you will see they will quickly relieve themselves. The bitch should be handed the puppies back, rear end towards her, and hopefully she will then continue her maternal duties. Very occasionally you will get a bitch that does not clean the puppies readily. You will have to encourage her to do so. Failing this, it is a job you will have to do until the pups undertake the task themselves.

After a day or two the umbilical cord dries up and falls off. Sometimes, if the bitch has been unduly zealous with the puppies, she can cause a hernia at the site of the umbilical. If small, hernias usually will close of their own accord. Sometimes, however, hernias are hereditary and may need surgical

correction at a later date. Your vet will advise as and when necessary.

Dehydration in a puppy can be caused through loose motions. If a puppy is limp and listless, immediately call a vet. There is a condition called fading puppy syndrome where puppies, usually at some time during the first ten days, seem suddenly to give up on life for no apparent reason. They become too weak to suckle, they start to dehydrate and they feel clammy to the touch. They whine and cry a lot and their temperature rises. Once set on this path, there is little you can do to retrieve them. There seems to be no concrete reason why this happens. It may be that the mother's milk is inferior, although initially it has seemed to be fine. We once had a litter of Boxers, six in all, that died, one after the other, over a period of four days. All the veterinary attention in the world apparently has no effect once puppies get on this slippery slide.

Puppies begin to teethe at around three weeks, and they then begin to suck on anything – quite often it is on their litter-mates' ears, legs or penises. They should be discouraged from doing so, as they can cause soreness and damage to their siblings.

LEAVING HOME
At about eight weeks of age the puppies are ready to go into their new homes. They are feeding well and have learned many of the social graces that will endear them to their new family. If you have any doubts about letting a puppy go, then a couple more weeks of individual tuition can only be for the better. Running a puppy on is not a problem if you are keeping one from the litter yourself. But

do remember, it makes it harder to part with a pup the older he gets, for they are all individuals and each has his own way of captivating you.

The puppies will all have been registered with the Kennel Club and you should have the registration documents on hand for the new owners, as well as the transfer of ownership form, which you will have completed and signed. A five-generation pedigree should also be ready for the new owners. You will also need to provide a comprehensive diet sheet and a list of the injections which have been given and the dates, plus the name of the worming formula. I also enclose a list of do's and dont's with regard to the puppy.

I will have had my vet check all the puppies over before they leave. He will have checked for eye problems, slipping patellas, mouths, hernias, heart and lungs and the pup's general physical condition.

I prefer new owners to collect their new puppies in the mornings, especially if they have to travel on long journeys. The pup will have been fed a light meal. Bad experiences of journeys can form a pattern for the future. Though the pup will have been taken out and about prior to leaving us, it will usually have been in the company of other puppies. With his new owners it is preferable that his initial experiences with them are good ones, thus his first journey must be as trouble-free as possible. Feeling sick and throwing up on the back seat would not be conducive to this. Travelling on an empty stomach is never a good idea, so,

as I mentioned before, just a light meal, time to relieve himself, then a calm transfer to the car and he is on his way. A tense and apprehensive atmosphere will transmit to the puppy – the Shiba at any age is very attuned to those around him. His perception of the world around him is very acute.

You will, of course, be very upset at the pup's going, but I always reassure myself with the fact that he is (in most cases) going into a family where he will be the centre of their world and he does not have to share that love with any other dog. He will have it all to himself. Arrangements should be made to see him from time to time, but not within the following few months, for he will need to have space and time to bond to his new people. Have the new owners phone you and let you know that they have all arrived home safely. Periodic telephone calls from them, just to let you know he is settling in and progressing well, are helpful. It is important that the new owners feel free to phone you if, at any time, they are unsure about the puppy. This way you can help and support them for the benefit of the puppy. The greatest thrill will come when you see that puppy again at a future date and you see him looking fit, well and happy, and for sure he will recognise you. Though it was a relatively short period of time that he spent in the nest, it was an important time in the puppy's development and it will have had a far-reaching effect on his long-term well-being.

11 HEALTH CARE AND INHERITED CONDITIONS

As a breed the Shiba seems to be very fit and healthy, with very few inherent problems. However, the following are some conditions to look out for. If you are in any doubt about your Shiba's health, consult your vet immediately.

SKIN PROBLEMS
The symptoms start with the Shiba scratching and continually licking itself on a particular spot; it can be on the back at the base of the tail; it can be on its thighs either side of its anus. It can be on its legs, at the base of its ears or even around its mouth. While one's first impressions are that it has been taken over by unwelcome visitors – fleas – this is not usually the case. It seems to be more a hormonal condition. It is a common occurrence in the Shiba and one to watch out for. Early detection can

The Shiba is a hardy breed and should suffer few health problems.

perhaps lessen the time it takes to cure the problem. The area quickly loses hair and the skin underneath begins to go very pink and then darkens and discolours. Your vet's urgent attention is required. There are a number of creams that work but it is a question of finding the one that works on your particular dog. Some vets will use an anthistamine injection, which also has some good results.

Young Shibas sometimes also suffer with a 'nappy rash' condition, or heat rash, which also will need attention from your vet. There seems to be no sure-fire answer to these conditions in the Shiba. It is more a question of finding out just what works for your dog.

SLIPPING PATELLAS

Also known as luxating patellas, this is when the knee-cap slips out of place and becomes weakened in the process. It is usually caused through a loose ligament, or too shallow a groove in the bone holding the knee cap. It can be an hereditary problem and if so, these animals should be discarded from breeding programmes. It can also be caused by an injury. While it does not always cause distress to the dog, it can cause wear on the knee-cap and result in the knee-cap becoming holed. However, this is more likely to occur in heavier breeds of dogs.

PROGRESSIVE RETINAL ATROPHY

All Shibas should be eye-tested regularly for PRA, which is an eye condition which eventually can cause blindness. Eye clinics are held regularly by qualified vets for the detection of this unpleasant hereditary condition. The examinations are painless and simple. The dog should be examined annually up until the age of six years before it can be considered clear with any degree of certainty. Any dog showing signs should be eliminated from breeding programmes.

HIP DYSPLASIA

This is not, at present, a breed problem in the Shiba. Nevertheless, breeding stock should be hip X-rayed and scored. Dogs scored high should not be bred from. HD, as it is commonly known, is more prevalent in heavy breeds. While many people consider it to be an hereditary problem, many others consider it to be an environmental and a rearing problem. It would appear that dogs with bad hip joints produce bad hip-jointed dogs. But, conversely, good hip-jointed dogs do not always produce good hips, though they, of course, have a greater chance of producing structurally sound progeny. HD will eventually cause a great deal of pain to the affected dog and will make it lame. X-rays should be taken at a year plus, and, more important, before mating a bitch and before a male is used at stud, to determine whether they are suitable to be bred from.

MONORCHIDS AND CRYPTORCHIDS

Monorchids are males with only one testicle descended. While they may breed normally, the retained testicle is infertile and any resulting progeny may carry infertility problems. The retained testicle has a very high percentage rate of becoming cancerous, thus endangering the dog's life. Cryptorchids have no

132

testicles and are not able to produce off-spring. The Shiba male can be very slow in maturing in this particular aspect. I have known a male to be 10 months of age before both testicles had descended. The testicles descending around seven months of age is not unusual in the Shiba. Some Shiba males do seem to have the power to retract their testicles. It has been said that if there are other alpha males around, the youngsters are in no hurry to prove their maleness and to seem, in doing so, to challenge the alpha dog.

DROP EARS
It should be said that this is a very rare condition in Shibas and while sometimes the ears may be slow to rise, I have not seen a Shiba with ears totally down. Occasionally you may see a Shiba with a floppy ear at half-mast but again, this is a rarity.

THE LONG COAT
The gene that produces the long coat is present in the Shiba. From time to time a puppy will appear in a litter with a long coat where, previously, there have been

none. You can go several generations without a long coat, then out of the blue, one will appear. They are usually even more beautiful and cuddly to look at. The coat is longer and usually much softer and the dogs have feathering on the ears and legs. The tail is extra bushy with longer hair. While this coat is no problem to the dogs, they cannot – or should not – be exhibited in the show ring. But as pets they are adorable.

SPAYING OR NEUTERING
If you decide that you do not wish to breed from your dog or bitch then spaying or neutering is the answer. From the dog or bitch's point of view it has no adverse effects on their well-being, and in many cases makes life easier for all concerned. It will not alter their personalities, and it may well settle them down, for the dog will not have the urge to roam or fight to maintain his status and the female will not have the encumbrance of being confined because of her seasons. Weight gain is perhaps the only consideration. The necessary surgery is both simple and painless and recuperation is speedy. Your vet will advise you as to the optimum time when these procedures should be undertaken.

PARVOVIRUS
This is an horrendous disease that can strike at any time, though it is more likely to affect those dogs that have not been vaccinated against it. Young puppies are especially vulnerable. No-one knows for sure how it is transmitted, but it is thought most likely to be airborne. It can wipe out a litter of puppies in days. Even older dogs have to put up a real battle to fight it. Sadly, it usually

The longcoated Shiba is incorrect according to the Breed Standard, but it makes a very attractive pet dog.

leaves the survivor with a weakness. First signs are a foul-smelling, bloody diarrhoea accompanied by sickness and listlessness. The dog becomes dehydrated very quickly. Immediate veterinary attention is required. Identifying the disease early is the key to saving your Shiba. If he shows any signs of the symptoms, do not delay – consult your vet. Puppies do initially receive maternal antibodies from their mother but vaccinations should be given early, on the advice of your vet.

CYSTITIS AND VAGINITIS
These are conditions that sometimes affect bitches, whether puppy or adult. Cystitis is the very frequent passing of urine – or straining and not passing urine. Vaginitis is the appearance of a sticky discharge or pus. Both ailments require medication. A constant supply of fresh drinking water and a clean, stress-free environment are essential.

EAR DISORDERS
Ear trouble is usually indicated by the dog shaking its head (this is *NOT* to be confused with the Shiba Shake mentioned in the Dog Showing chapter) or rubbing its head along the ground. It is most commonly caused by ear mites or an infection. A vet's check is necessary to determine which.

ENTROPION AND TRICHIASIS
These are hereditary diseases. They may appear in a puppy as early as six weeks of age, but then right themselves when the skull has developed. Entropion is the turning-in of the eyelids. Mild entropion can be dealt with by using an ointment as directed by your vet. More severe cases

may need surgery. Trichiasis is where the eyelashes are growing inwards and irritating the eye. Whichever condition prevails, you should not delay in consulting your vet, for the rubbing on the eyeball of either hair or skin can be extremely painful to your dog. The pressure on the cornea can cause ulcers, which in turn cause blindness.

DISTEMPER
Signs of this disease are loss of appetite, chills, depression and a fever. It usually affects young dogs but of course all dogs are susceptible to the disease. In the advanced stages it affects the lungs, the intestines and the nervous system. At the first signs it should be treated immediately. If a dog recovers he may well be left with a paralysis, have convulsions or have some other spastic type of defect, for example twitching. Inoculations are vital in puppyhood, with an annual booster thereafter.

LEPTOSPIROSIS
Infection is caused by either Canicola or Copenhageni and this can be picked up by the dog if he licks substances contaminated by the urine or faeces of infected animals. Brown rats are the main carriers of this disease. The first signs of contamination are vomiting, weakness and a yellowish discoloration of the jaws, teeth and tongue, which is caused by the kidney being infected. Treatment is by having your vet administer the bacterins to protect your dog from the disease. The frequency of the doses is governed by the risk factor involved.

CANINE HEPATITIS

Signs of this disease are drowsiness, loss of appetite, a high temperature and a great thirst. Vomiting may occur. Other signs to look for are swelling of the neck, head and abdomen. This disease is quick-acting and death may occur in just a few hours after contracting it. Inoculation in puppyhood followed by an annual booster is recommended.

KENNEL COUGH

This is highly contagious and affects the dog's upper respiratory tract. All dogs are susceptible to kennel cough and the spread of the disease in a kennel is vicious. However, it is not just confined to dogs in kennels. First signs are a hacking type of cough, with mucus, and with high fever. Early veterinary treatment is essential. Though a serious disease in dogs, it lasts for only a week or two, and if cured usually leaves no adverse reactions.

PARASITES

A parasite is an animal that lives in, or on, another species of animal – the host animal. The parasite gains from the encounter while the host suffers and reacts to the intrusion. Many skin problems in the dog are attributed to parasites. Fleas are the most common cause of the major proportion of skin problems. The female flea can lay hundreds of eggs and these mature in less than three weeks. The ears of the dog are the fleas' favourite habitat, as is the base of the tail and around the dog's neck. Fleas also lurk in crevices, carpets and bedding. While treating the dog, remember to treat his surroundings at the same time in order to eradicate the

fleas. There are thousands of different types of fleas that cause many different types of diseases. There are numerous products available to use in the eradication of fleas. There are also pill programmes available, which can be administered monthly to your dog, that prevent flea invasion of your pet. Consult your vet for more details.

Ticks can cause your dog serious problems. They adhere themselves to vegetation in the countryside and wooded areas and, as animals pass, they attach themselves to the animal. The whole of the tick has to be removed from the dog to prevent any serious problem developing. To remove ticks you need to grasp the whole of the visible part of the tick – its head will be buried inside the skin of the dog – between your thumbnail and your index fingernail, as close to the dog's skin as possible. Then turn it and pull it out, hopefully removing it all. Or you can use a pair of tweezers if you are at home. I have been told that a lighted cigarette applied to the tick will make it release itself quickly, but I have never tried this and would be loath to try it on a coated breed such as the Shiba. If you cannot extricate the tick, then get your vet to show you how to do it.

In England the roundworm is the most common worm found in dogs and other animals. It appears as a long creamy-coloured worm around two to three inches in length. The dog usually passes them in a cluster. Your vet will supply worming tablets and the dosage is measured according to the dog's size. I always administer these pills on an empty stomach, usually first thing in the morning, about an hour or so before the dog is fed. This then gives the tablets time to work without the addition of food in the stomach. It also gives the dog time to pass the worms throughout the day, before he is settled down for the night. Ten days later a further dose of tablets will clear up any lingering worms that have formed.

Tapeworm is also quite common and, again, veterinary treatment is needed to eradicate them. The sign of tapeworm is strange-looking segments in the dog's faeces. When wormed, the tapeworm will break up inside the dog, and will be passed out with the faeces. When worming I keep the dogs on concrete, not grass, and segregate them from each other, so that there is no risk of one dog infecting another dog. Also, you can then be sure that the worms have been cleared from each dog individually.

Hookworm and whipworm are other types of worm infestations. A laboratory test on the dog's stool can assist in deciding on the best treatment to pursue. Heartworm is passed on to dogs by mosquitoes and is usually found in tropical countries, although there have been incidences in other areas. Affected dogs seem listless, have difficulty breathing and lose weight despite seeming to have a hearty appetite. Giving a preventative medicine through the spring, summer and autumn is advisable. Your vet must first take a blood sample to determine the presence of disease. If your dog is free from infestation, then he can be given a preventative medicine to maintain his health. The heartworm life-cycle is as follows: a carrier mosquito bites a dog and deposits microfilaria, which then travel through the dog's bloodstream and lodge in the heart, where they reproduce. The carrier dog is then bitten by another mosquito, which consequently becomes infected. That mosquito, in its turn, goes on to bite an uninfected dog, who then contracts the disease. And thus the heartworm spreads.

DENTAL CARE
A constant check should be kept on your Shiba's teeth. In puppyhood, when the milk teeth begin to be replaced by the adult teeth, it is most important to check, weekly, that the milk teeth are being shed and the adult teeth are growing in the right place. Sometimes the milk teeth are retained and the adult teeth grow behind or alongside them, and this can cause problems. This is quite common in small breeds of dogs. Malocclusion – a bad bite – can result if the milk teeth are retained. If the incisor teeth are retained this can certainly result in a bad bite. The most commonly retained teeth are the canines.

By eight weeks the puppy should have 28 teeth. A shortage of milk teeth does not necessarily mean that he will not have all his adult teeth. By eight months the Shiba's adult teeth should have arrived. 42 teeth are a full complement. Teething can vary from Shiba to Shiba, and adult teeth can go on appearing up until twelve to fourteen months of age.

Discoloration of teeth in the puppy may occur, due to malnutrition resulting from a severe case of worms, from a lack of vitamin D, or from a calcium/phosphate imbalance, and ugly brownish-black rings may also appear. This condition is known as 'distemper teeth'. Damaged teeth, ones that are cracked or broken, should always be

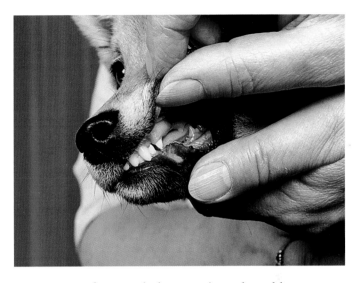

Check your puppy's teeth on a regular basis.

Photo: John Daniels.

checked, for they can cause unnecessary pain and discomfort to your Shiba. Shibas are not very accommodating when it comes to dental inspections but, with the need to keep problems at bay, you will have to practise, from birth, the teeth inspection procedure. Dental cleaning is another good way of overcoming this problem. Though perhaps unnecessary, a daily brushing of the teeth will become a habit that is tolerated by your Shiba, along with his general grooming programme.

THE OLDER SHIBA

Old age creeps up on us all, and has no mercy, whether you are animal or human. With the ageing process a gradual degeneration occurs. You may not always be aware of its onset in your dog. Remember that is roughly considered that one year in the dog's life-cycle is equivalent to seven in the human's. At the age of seven your dog is well into middle age. He may become less active and not eat as well as he did, but his thirst increases. He may

frequently be constipated, and he may need to urinate more frequently as his bladder slackens. As he slows up he may gain weight and become obese. Extremes of heat and cold become more intolerable to him and he may tire more quickly. His hearing and sight may become impaired, and his general good humour and temperament may recede slightly. Other medical ailments that may occur are arthritis, rheumatism, kidney infections and heart disease – all ailments that will require veterinary attention and treatment at their onset.

On a more gloomy note, the time will come when your companion has to leave you. It may be a decision that you have to make or, hopefully, one that just happens with the passing of time. Every living creature has its own dignity and this should always be uppermost in your mind. When the quality of life becomes intolerable or unacceptable, then you have to make that decision for your loved one. He has, after all, always given you without question his love, loyalty and trust. You must be trusted to know

137

At nine years of age, this Shiba still has plenty of energy.

when enough is enough. I could never allow any animal of mine to face the end without being there with him to comfort and support him. Though an unbearable task, both for the vet and for you, the only consolation is that it is swift and painless for your dog. I insist on being with my dog until he has gone – it is the least I can do. Understandably, not everyone can handle the situation. If you are going to unnerve the dog, then do not stay. If you wish to have your dog cremated, this can be arranged through your vet beforehand. Alternatively, if you wish him to buried in your garden, then this should also be arranged beforehand. Most vets will come to the house to administer the injection. This is the least traumatic for your Shiba, for the surroundings are familiar and comforting to him and it is, after all, his home .

VETERINARY HOMEOPATHY
Homeopathy is essentially a natural healing process with three basic principles:
1) That a medicine which, in large doses, produces symptoms of a disease will, in small doses, cure the disease.
2) That by using an extreme dilution, the medicine's curative properties are enhanced and all the poisonous or undesirable side-effects are lost.
3) That homeopathic medicines are prescribed individually by studying the whole animal.
A large proportion of homeopathic remedies are plant-based and there is a wide range. They look exactly the same as medicines and can be in the form of

granules, tablets, liquids, ointments or suppositories. The following is a list of the more well-known, most used and successful remedies. Alternative medicine is becoming more popular.

Arnica for bruising, sprains and swelling, shock before and after operations and for the after-effects of tooth extractions.

Rhus tox is used in conditions of rheumatism and arthritis which are worse after rest but improve after exercise.

Calendula lotion for bathing wounds and sores.

Apis Mel for insect bites and stings and injuries where there is swelling with fluid present.

Hypericum is a useful pain killer. Use for bruised bones or nerves, for lacerated wounds and deep puncture bites, and after operations.

Caudophyllum is for use in the later stages of pregnancy or birth complications and for the reduction of puppies' stress. If given to the bitch in the later stages of pregnancy, it is passed into the puppies through the placenta and gives them a boost to cope with the birth process, which can sometimes take quite a long time.

Garlic gives excellent all-round benefits if given daily. It is especially good for cleaning through the body system.

12 THE JAPANESE SHIBA INU IN BRITAIN

In the summer of 1985 three Shibas were imported into the UK from Arizona, USA, by Kath and Gerald Mitchell of the Kiskas kennels. These kennels are famous for their Akitas, and it is true to say that if you love the Akita you will adore the Shiba – it is a natural progression. Kath and Gerald were no exception. After seeing the Shiba on one of their trips to the States they were captivated, and the introduction of this

adorable breed to Britain had begun.

The three Shibas came from the famous Jade-Shogun kennels owned by Terry and Ed Arndt. Terry was a founder member of the Shiba Ken Club in America in the early days of the breed's introduction there. One of the three Shibas was the bitch Shogun Hisui Megami, who was to be the foundation of Kath and Brian Hindley's Yorlands Shiba kennels. The other two were

The first group photo of all the Shibas out of quarantine, November 1987.

Shogun Hisui Yukitamahime, a bitch with the pet name of Dixie, and her litter brother, Shogun Hisui Yukihikari, called Yen, who were kept by the Mitchells. They were released from quarantine in February 1986 and their first public appearance was on television in a pre-Crufts programme.

The Hindleys, like myself, had many years of experience through breeding and exhibiting Rottweilers prior to the Shiba. In 1986 the Mitchells brought in a further bitch from the States, Ogan No Takame Ogon Taiyo So of Kiskas. When she arrived she was in whelp. She had been mated to Beni Washi-go, who was owned by Terry Arndt; they shared the same sire, Shi Shi. She whelped two bitches in quarantine, Kiskas Cinnamon at Madason, pet-named Ski, who came to live with me, and Kiskas Whisper, who stayed at Kiskas.

Tamawakamaru of Madason: The first Japanese import to the UK, who came via the USA.

THE FIRST BRITISH-BORN SHIBAS

Also in 1986 Yen and Dixie were mated and two bitches and a dog were born – Kiskas Jack Daniels, Anniaka, and Tokyo Rose, known as Tammy. She went to Bill and Jennie Cowland and was Kerrilands' foundation bitch; Anniaka (Nikki) joined me at the Madason kennels. That litter arrived on October 14th. However, the first litter of Shibas to be born in England was on September 7th 1986 and it was bred by Kath Hindley. The sire was Shogun Hisui Yukihikari at Kiskas (Yen) and the dam was Shogun Hisui Megami of Yorlands. Two puppies resulted, a male and a female

A further event in 1986 was the arrival of the first Japanese-born male into the UK. He was imported by me, again from the USA, and was called

Tamawakamaru of Madason (Taka). He was bred by Mr Yaichiro Watatsu in Japan. He was taken into America and then Terry Arndt allowed us to have him and bring him to England, where his impact on the breed was immense. He was the first Shiba to go through the Kennel Club BVA hip scoring scheme with a 0/0 score. Sparskip Spartan, owned by Lyn Lane, is the only other 0/0 hip scoring Shiba. At the first showing of the Shibas at Crufts, in 1992, Tamawakamaru took the Reserve Dog Ticket, alongside his daughter Madason Toya who was Best Bitch in Breed. John and Dana Ogilvie imported a female, Camboaljo Ujahjme (Suki), early in 1987. She was of the colour described as sesame.

Kiskas Tokyo Rose.   *Photo: Lyn Lane.*   *Kiskas Jack Daniels.*

EXTENDING THE COLOUR RANGE

Thus far the Shibas that had arrived in the UK had all been reds. Then Betty and Joe Neath imported a black and tan bitch called Minimeadows Summer Dream. Later she was to be mated to the Swedish dog brought in by the Hindleys called Beni Kiku Go (a red), which resulted in a bumper litter of seven puppies born in the autumn of 1987.

Another significant import, also a black and tan, came from Japan. It was Roy Mulligan's and Mr Kadawaki's Kurachime of Dongayamasow. I saw her at the age of nine in a Veteran class and thought how well she looked and that she was of such good type. While in quarantine she produced a litter containing Makota Aka Danshaku, a really strong red, who is behind several kennel lines now in the UK. He was later joined by two further Japanese imports, namely Japanese Champion Juho of Suishoen, a brilliant red, and Kuretetsu of Kohtokusow, another black and tan. 1988 saw the arrival of Yukarihime of Mikado House, imported by Ann Shimwell of the Wellshim kennels. Sadly Ann died before seeing the remarkable success her home-bred Wellshim Blackjack had in the breed. Ann's son Chris carries on her success.

Several other imports followed, but these initial ones carried the burden of laying the foundations of the Shiba in England and, in hindsight, they did a really good job! As had happened before in other countries, the Shibas captivated all in their path, gaining admirers and fanciers. Whenever and wherever the Shibas appeared they usually took centre stage, frequently being mistaken for little foxes.

142

KENNEL CLUB CAUTION

The Kennel Club was a little more cautious. Registrations were accepted onto the registration lists and registration documents supplied, but the breed was place in an Import Register, which was an innovation by the Kennel Club at that time. The Shibas were joined by the Polish Lowland dog and there they all remained for several years. The Kennel Club wished new breeds to have a low profile, in order to give them time to develop and standardise. It also gave the breeds time to build on their gene pools. This meant that the Shiba could only be shown in 'Import Classes', so a Shiba who won through in an Import Register Class could not compete with other Best of Breed Winners for Best in Show – though many Show Managers did allow a lap of honour when an Import Register dog won through its classification, thus giving the breed some exposure to would-be enthusiasts and fanciers, of which there were many.

At that time there were many breeders in other breeds who, though more than a little interested in the Shiba, took a step back and waited just to see where the breed was going. It fell to a small minority of dedicated lovers of the Shiba to take the breed forward and to promote its virtues, as well as making people aware of its vices. Today's Shibas in England owe much to these people.

COMPETING ON EQUAL TERMS

In hindsight I personally feel the Kennel Club's decision to keep the new breeds in a low profile situation was an excellent course of action. The restriction stayed until October 1990, at which time the breed was allowed to have its own breed classes and hold its own Breed show. The first breed show took place in October 1991. The honour of judging went to

Azgard Koko San: First Irish Champion bitch, and first Junior Warrant bitch.

143

Madason Toya: Best Bitch Crufts 1992.

Photo: John Hartley.

Les Crawley, Founder President of the Club. Les gave Best In Show to Janet Campion's Makoto Tobias Chevawn, a worthy winner who sired numerous show winners.

The Shiba was then also allowed to compete on equal terms with other breeds and challenge for Best in Group and Best in Show, an achievement that the breed very quickly attained – all the more remarkable when you think of how young the breed was in England.

Some notable firsts were: in 1991 Wellshim Blackjack is Vormund won the Utility Group at LKA in Birmingham; Madason Fanfare went Best in Show at the All Breeds Open Show; and Azgard Kishuu from Abkass took the Puppy Stakes at Darlington Championship Show. In 1992 Kerrilands Total Eclipse won Reserve Best Puppy in Show in the South Wales Championship Show, and in 1996 Ch. Vormund I'm Smartie took Best In Show at Richmond In 1991 the first Shiba to gain his Junior warrant was Farmbrook Hot Gossip, who was bred by Chris Thomas and owned by Tony Walker.

Classes for the Shiba were given at Crufts (without Challenge Certificates) in 1992; the judging honour went to Mrs Jo Gibbs (Merryn) who gave the Best Dog and Best of Breed to Liz Dunhill's Welshim Black Jack is Vormund and my own Madason Toya, who took Best Bitch. Black Jack went on to many successes. He was an outstanding black and tan dog who filled the eye with his presence and stature. Black Jack did much to promote the breed, and he was always handled to perfection by his expert handler/owner, Lizzie. Sadly, he left the country before Champion status was approved by the Kennel Club for the breed. He now resides in France, where he gained his International crown.

THE SHIBA BREED CLUB

At the beginning of 1987, with a great deal of interest being shown in the breed, it was felt that a Club should be established, and so I arranged a meeting of some forty or so Shiba fanciers at my home. The meeting expressed the wish that the Kennel Club should be approached for permission to have a Club. On contact with the Kennel Club they suggested that an Inaugural meeting should be held. Advertisements were placed in the Dog Press and the inaugural meeting took place in April 1987 at Bledlow Ridge in Buckinghamshire. From the people attending, a provisional Shiba Club was set up. The meeting proposed that a committee be set up with Les Crawley as Chairman. Les is a very well-known Boxer breed specialist. He had been instrumental in the early days of The Siberian Huskies Club formation and had much expertise in all aspects of dogdom. He hosted the Crufts previews on television for several years and, along with his judging and showing, had a radio spot. The Treasurer was Vi Todd who has bred Shih-Tzus for many many years, and I was Secretary.

The Kennel Club registered the Provisional Shiba Club in November 1987. There was a great deal of work to be done and we were fortunate that many of our founder members had served on committees and run shows before and many gave of their time and expertise unstintingly. A Newsletter was established in September 1987. The editor was Alan Matthews of the Holker kennels. Alan's task was a very difficult one in those early day as communications with Japan were

Burwen Wild 'n' Wicked pictured after winning her first CC at Birmingham 1997 under breed pioneer Kath Mitchell.
Photo: Carol Ann Johnson.

Nakayu go Kazusa Nakansow: Imported from Japan by Jill Knight Messenger – the first Japanese native import to win a Group at a Championship show.

The Contest of Champions: Kiskas Jack Daniels and Madason Beaujolais at Merryn represented the breed.

extremely difficult, due mainly to the language barrier. The Shiba was allowed a column of breed notes under the Rare Breed section on a weekly basis in both *Dog World* and *Our Dogs*, so we were able to keep information flowing about the breed as it came to hand from wherever and whenever new information was received. Membership of the Club grew.

Seminars and teach-ins, together with eye clinics and breed awareness days, were held in several parts of the country. The first Shiba showcase followed the Annual General Meeting at Bledlow Ridge in March 1988, and the following year there was one at Kegworth in the Midlands. We were fortunate enough to have awakened the interest of many well-known dog people, so that they came along to see and learn about the Shiba, in addition to giving their contributions on general dog topics.

Judges' teach-in days were held. The idea behind these was to give judges who were already experienced in other breeds the opportunity of seeing the Shiba and to learn the finer points about the breed in an informal and friendly atmosphere. The teach-ins were also available to owners, breeders and exhibitors so that they could go over and assess the Shiba before undertaking judging appointments. It also helped the Club to formulate a Judging List for the breed. As well as learning days there were social get-togethers, which began with a barbecue after the Open Show at Evesham, where some 30 Shibas had been entered, followed by Christmas Socials.

From the initial three Shibas imported in 1985 the breed grew and had 180-plus registrations at the Kennel Club in 1989. Two Open Shows a Year were allowed by the Kennel Club and this gave everyone the opportunity to observe the breed and its progression. The Club was lucky to have had a nucleus of well-seasoned and knowledgeable Breeder/Exhibitors/Judges at its inception, who set the foundation for its success. Registrations of the Shiba increased at a steady rate, as did the interest in the breed.

SHIBA CHAMPIONS

The Shiba was invited to take part in The Contest of Champions Show held in Wembley, although at that time they had not received Championship status. The breed's representatives were the dog Kiskas Jack Daniels, owned by Kath and Gerald Mitchell, and a bitch owned by Jo Gibbs of the Merryn kennels, Madason Beaujolais at Merryn. In 1996 the Kennel Club granted the Shiba Inu Challenge Certificates – the first was awarded at Crufts; the other shows allowed to make the Awards were Birmingham National, Scotland, The Welsh Kennel Club and British Utility Breeds Association

The first male to be made up to a Champion was Kerrilands Total Majic owned and bred by Jenny and Bill Cowland, and the first female was Vormund I'm Smartie owned and bred by Liz Dunhill. To attain Championship status in England the dog has to win outright in its sex classes at a Championship Show. That means that if it is a bitch it must beat all the other Shiba bitches exhibited on that day and be Best Bitch in Breed, and the males must beat all the other males. When a dog has attained this eminence on three separate occasions, under three different judges, the Kennel Club will award the Champion's certificate. The Champion can then only compete in the Open class for the breed or in Champion Stakes classes for All Breeds.

THE KERRILANDS KENNELS

Bill and Jenny Cowland, who made up that first male Shiba Champion in

Ch. Kerrilands Total Majic: The first British male Champion.

147

England, were introduced to the Japanese Shiba Inu by Gerald and Kath Mitchell in 1986. They acquired their first bitch from them. She was called Kiskas Tokyo Rose at Kerrilands. In 1987 a male joined her.

Later on in 1987 they imported a bitch which was to have a great influence on their Shiba kennels. She arrived from California and her name was Shogun Kiki at Kerrilands. Kiki produced the main foundation bitch in their kennels, who was called Kerrilands Bianca.

She was a white bitch who, when correctly mated into strong Japanese lines, eventually produced some of the generations which resulted in the first English Shiba Champion. He was an orange red male with the correct markings and was Ch. Kerrilands Total Majic. Bill and Jenny had both worked so hard with the breed to achieve success that it is difficult to express the joy they felt when Majic won his title.

Bill and Jenny were founder members of the Japanese Shiba Inu Club of Great Britain. Bill was treasurer for several years and also served on the committee. Their involvement with the Shiba spans a decade and they feel that much progress has been made, as can be seen from the fine examples in today's show ring, and that although there is still a long way to go the breed is heading in the right direction.

THE MADASON KENNELS

As a small child my father always promised me a dog but those were the war years. It was not until I was married and had my own home that I was able to make the promise come true.

That was in 1958, when I purchased my first Boxer, Butch, a large brindle male, and a love affair with pedigree dogs began. Butch was a lovely dog, good with children and a trustworthy companion but not destined for great things.

In the early sixties I purchased another male, Brutus, this time with a view to showing him, which I did with limited success. It was around this time that I registered my prefix Madason, which was derived from the first two letters of my Christian name Maureen, and the same with my husband's name David, and the last three letters of our surname. For the next ten years I bred and showed Boxers and undertook several judging appointments.

Then in the early 70s I was smitten with the Rottweiler breed, with whom I had considerable success.

However, in 1985 when the Japanese Shiba Inu was first introduced to this country, I was totally captivated by the breed and, as I have said earlier, I purchased, from the Kiskas Kennels, a puppy bitch from their first mating. Another bitch was brought in from Arizona in 1986 in whelp and I had a female from that litter. I also had in quarantine from America at that time Tamawakamaru of Madason.

At Crufts in 1992, where Shibas had classes for the first time, I took the Best Bitch award with my homebred bitch Madason Toya and Reserve Best Dog. My greatest honour was to judge the Shiba Inu at Crufts in 1994, which I did in traditional Japanese costume.

It was a memorable occasion, one that has gone down in the breed's history.

Maureen Atkinson pictured with Gingseng Aru de Vaudeville – 'Nicco'.
Photo: Banbury Guardian.

Sparskip Sparkler (Nedraw Cathay to Sparskip – Ginseng Aru de Vaudeville).
Photo: Martin Leigh.

THE SPARSKIP KENNELS

Lyn Lane's involvement with dogs stems from the Pembroke Corgi which she had as a teenager, followed by a succession of English Springer Spaniels. Her love-affair with the Shiba began when she saw pictures of the early imports into England. Subsequently, when attending a show, she found herself at the ringside of the Shibas, where she was asked to hold on to one of these foxy creatures while its owner was in the ring exhibiting another. Captivated by the unique Shiba gaze, Lyn then began her search for her special puppy. After visiting several breeders, in October 1988 she became the proud owner of Madason Marcasite at Sparskip, known as Zeta. She was from Kiskas Cinnamon at Madason and Tamawakamaru of Madason. She has never been bred, though not for want of trying, and is still going strong at nine years. She is still being shown successfully in Veteran classes. There are now several other Shibas in the fold, including the outstanding black, tan and white Gingseng Aru de Vaudeville, imported in partnership from Belgium. Lyn has been a member of the Japanese Shiba Inu Club of Great Britain from its early days and has served on its committee.

13 THE SHIBA INU IN NORTH AMERICA

It is believed that the first Shiba entered America in 1954, taken in by a serviceman returning from Japan after his tour of duty. 1977 saw the arrival of the second Shiba, followed by many more as their popularity grew. The first litter born in the United States was in 1979. The sire and dam were imports owned by Julia Cadwell.

THE AKC CRITERIA
The Shiba Inu was classified as a 'Rare Breed' of dog in America, a designation that creates an eighth group for show purposes, along with the seven groups already recognized by the American Kennel Club (AKC). Though the Shiba is registered in most countries under the jurisdiction of the FCI, the American Kennel Club did not accept the Shiba onto its register readily. Various criteria had to be met. A national parent club had to maintain a register and that club had to show there was a nationwide interest in the breed, with growing activity. The National Shiba Club of America was set up in 1983, having grown out of the Shiba Club of America.

Registration and stud books were maintained. Once the NSCA had satisfied the American Kennel Club's criteria, the AKC permitted the Shiba to enter Miscellaneous Classes in 1992, at which time some 1,200 dogs were registered. In the early days Japanese registration was necessary before the Shiba could be registered with a club.

JAPANESE ASSISTANCE
The American fanciers are fortunate in that Japan is relatively closer to their shores than to ours. They are able to visit more easily and get their fill of the Shiba Inu in its native country. However, Japanese breeders, having brought the Shiba back from extinction, are naturally reluctant to part with their best dogs – and rightly so, when you realise the struggle they had to perpetuate their 'Natural Treasure'.

The relatively close proximity of Japan has meant that the American show scene has been able to benefit from having Japanese judges officiating at their shows, who bring with them their vast knowledge of the breed. Information is easier to obtain, albeit there is still the language barrier to contend with. After having judged the breed, the visiting judge will give a lecture on the breed, usually at a banquet given in his honour.

THE AMERICAN KENNEL CLUB

The AKC was founded in September 1884. It is a non-profit organisation devoted to the advancement of pure-bred dogs. Its purpose is to adopt and enforce rules and regulations governing dog shows, Obedience trials, field trials and tracking tests and to foster and encourage interest in, and the health and welfare of, pure-bred dogs. The AKC is the major registry agency for pure-bred dogs in the United States and it publishes a monthly magazine *Pure Bred Dogs/American Kennel Gazette,* and a monthly *Stud Book Register* and other authoritative books.

Dog shows, hunting tests, lure coursing tests and trials are classed as tests of the dog's training or instinct, whereas Shows are evaluations of the dog's conformation. There are more than 11,000 events held under AKC License or sanctioned each year. Most parts of the country have one or more competitions every weekend. While most clubs advertise in their local papers, a list of events is published in each issue of the AKC *Gazette* Events Calendar. At the Shows judges compare the dogs in competition with their interpretation of the perfect dog described in the written Breed Standard. The dogs are also compared against each other and placed first to fourth. Most of the dogs are competing for points towards their Championship. It takes fifteen points including two majors – that is wins of

three, four or five points at a single show – under two different judges and a point under some third judge, to become a Champion of Record, indicated as Ch. before a dog's name. Points are awarded from one to five depending on the breed, the region in which the event takes place and the number of dogs and bitches actually in competition at a show. Judging is a process of elimination that ultimately results in one dog being selected Best in Show.

ENTERING A SHOW

Having seen a show advertised that you wish to enter, make contact with the show secretary who will send you a Premium List which includes class classification, the cost of entering the classes, the names of the judges officiating on the day and the trophies on offer. There will also be an official AKC entry form which has to be completed and returned with the entry fees. Shows are usually held lasting two or three days. Friday evening is usually given over to a seminar. Saturday is the day of the show, with a specialty banquet held on the Saturday evening at a nearby hotel. It all makes for a social and sporting weekend for dogs, owners and handlers alike.

On arrival at the show, judging programmes are available so you are able to follow the entries throughout the day. At unbenched shows you need only to be at the event at the time your breed is being judged.

THE AMERICAN SHOW SCENE

The show scene in America is vastly different to that of the UK. Puppies are able to compete at a much younger age than in England. From around three months of age they enter puppy walks and compete with each other. With vast distances to travel to and between shows, many Shibas are handled by professional handlers and they spend weeks travelling on the circuit.

To attain Championship status in America the dogs receive points towards their Championship. All dogs competing for Championship points are entered in one (or more) of the regular classes for their breed and sex. The classes are as follows:-

PUPPY: For dogs under one year. This may be divided into 6-9 months age group and 9-12 months.

NOVICE: For dogs not having won three firsts in Novice or any other classes, with the exception of puppy, nor of any Championship points.

BRED BY EXHIBITOR: For dogs not Champions owned wholly or partly by the breeder, and shown by him or a member of his family.

AMERICAN-BRED: For all dogs, except Champions, born in the USA, resulting from a mating which took place in the USA.

OPEN: For any dog.

(The same classes as shown for dogs above, apply to bitches.)

WINNERS CLASSES

WINNERS DOG: The first place winner of each class for males (which have not been beaten in any other class) compete for Winners Dog. He receives a purple ribbon and points in proportion to the number of males present.

RESERVE WINNERS DOG: The second place dog from the Winner Dog class competes with the dogs remaining in the ring, unless he has already been beaten by one of them, for Reserve Winners. The Reserve Winner receives a purple and white ribbon and moves up to winner if the Winner Dog is for any reason disqualified.

For bitches the same procedure as above applies.

BEST OF BREED: The Winners Dog and Winners Bitch compete with any champions entered for Best of Breed Entries in the Best of Breed class are dogs and bitches which are Champions, having acquired sufficient points in previous competitions. If there are no Champions entered, the Best of Winners is automatically Best of Breed. The other dog or bitch competing for Best of Winners is Best Opposite Sex. Winners of non-regular classes such as Veteran, Local or Field Dog (if they have not been previously defeated in a regular class) compete for Best of Breed. The Winner receives a purple and gold ribbon.

BEST OF WINNERS: If the Winners Dog or Bitch is awarded Best of Breed, it automatically is awarded Best of Winners, otherwise the Winners Dog and Winners Bitch are judged together for Best of Winners. In addition to the blue and white ribbon awarded, the Best of Winners may receive additional points if the opposite sex had an entry qualifying for higher points.

BEST OF OPPOSITE SEX: Following selection of Best of Breed and Best Winners all individuals of the sex opposite to Best of Breed remain in the ring. The Winners Dog or Bitch, whichever is also of the sex opposite to Best of Breed, is judged in this class. From this group Best of Opposite Sex is chosen. A red and white ribbon is awarded to the Best of Opposite Sex to Best of Breed.

THE GROUP: The Shiba belongs to the Working Group. The blue rosette for first in Group is given to the winner among all Best of Breed dogs competing in that particular group. Red, yellow and white rosettes are also given to the second, third and fourth place winners in Group.

BEST IN SHOW: The Group winners are judged for this top award. A rosette, coloured red, white and blue, is given.

NOTE: Four ribbons are awarded in each class, blue for first, red for second, yellow for third and white for fourth. Champions may compete in Puppy or Open classes, but are usually entered for Breed only, as they do not need the Championship points awarded to Winners Dog and Winners Bitch. To 'Finish' a dog means that he has achieved his Champion title. If a dog is 'Pointed',

this means that he has won 15 points plus two Majors under AKC rules. In order to receive a ROM (Register of Merit), a female has to have produced four Champions and a male has to have produced seven Champions.

THE SHIBA JOURNAL
A quarterly magazine called *The Shiba Journal* has been published for a number of years in the States. It is a truly magnificent and informative journal that has been avidly read throughout the world. Gretchen Haskett and Susan Houser who, in the early days, did the translations and the compiling of the information, have kept Shiba fanciers abreast of information as it arrived from Japan. As interest in the Shiba grows, and new people acquire the breed, the pool of information widens. Many Japanese breeders in America brought their knowledge and expertise of their

Int. SCA Nippo Ch. Beni Washi-Go.

Photo: Kohler.

native breed with them, thus benefiting us all.

THE JADE-SHOGUN KENNELS

Terry and Ed Arndt of the famous Jade-Shogun kennels were early pioneers of the breed in America. Their outstanding male in the early 1980s, Intl. Shiba Club of America, National Shiba Club of America Nippo Champion Beni Washi-Go, was an outstanding red who possessed an extremely outgoing personality. He loved people and did much to promote the breed. His glorious coat was perfect in texture, and he excelled in body and balance. He had outstanding movement. He was fifteen-and-a-half inches in height. Beni was the sire of some of our foundation stock in England. He produced, both here and in America, females of exceptional type, for example my Kiskas Cinnamon at Madason, who was from the litter of two females born in quarantine in England in November 1986.

Beni's kennelmate in those early days was Haru Sakura, known as Amber, an import who was full of type, with good angulation, although she was rather on the small size. Sadly Amber only had one litter before being spayed for medical reasons; however, she lived to a sprightly fifteen years of age. Terry continues to breed and has show-winning stock across the United States and into Canada. She is still very actively involved in seminars and Club promotions.

THE BLUE LOON KENNELS

Evelyn Behren of the Blue Loon Kennels, having researched the breed thoroughly in 1987, acquired her first Shiba in 1988. Evelyn's foundation male, Rare Breed Champion Tetsuryu of Hikari Kaidasow, apparently made quite a mark on the breed. He was a Japanese import and she acquired him when he was three years of age He is a Register of Merit Stud (ROM) and was the first to produce a ROM son, Ch. Hansha

Haru Sakura, known as Amber.

Photo: Terry Arndt.

ABOVE: Shogun's Nikko No Sunojo.

BELOW: Can. Ch. Sunjo's Seiu Sahsi Jo. Photo: Linda Lindt.

Remote Control. He has more than 50 Champion descendants throughout the United States. More important, Evelyn says "he's a family dog and rules their house at ten-and-a-half years of age."

THE FOXFIRE KENNELS

Another pioneer and innovator of the breed in America is Gretchen Haskett. She and her husband Tim are the famous Foxfire kennels. Gretchen's editorial prowess has been appreciated worldwide through the *Shiba Journal*. Her SCA Ch. Takishiido of Foxfire AKC SCA CD, is a lovely example of a black, tan and white Shiba, not only beautiful to look at, but with brains as well and the ability to gain a CD in working trials.

THE FOXTROT SHIBAS

Another early and extremely successful kennel was the Foxtrot Shibas of Kathy Brown and Bruce Truax. Kathy's expert handling, presentation and knowledgeable breeding programmes made her one of the outstanding breeders through the 1980s. NSCA and SCA Ch. Cowen's Patent Pending, known as 'Chaz', was a multi Best in Show Winner and one of Kathy's foundation Shibas, bred by Janice Cowen.

Kathy owned and successfully showed Ch. Hansha Remote Control, a Shiba with an outstanding Japanese head piece. He was a very successful sire. Known as R.C., he was bred by June Gilmore. A black, tan and white Japanese import of the Foxtrot kennels was Fukurimaru of Gunma Fukuda Kensha. Toy, as he was called, made quite an impact in the Foxtrot breeding programme. Foxtrot Shibas are

Am. Ch. Tetsuryu of Hikari Kaidasow (Japanese import).

Photo: Evelyn Behrens.

SCA Ch. Takishiido of Foxfire AK/SCA/CD.

Photo: Gretchen Haskett.

Fukurimaru of Gunma Fukuda Kensha (Japanese import): A significant sire for the Foxtrot kennel.   Photo: Foxtrot.

Am. Ch. Hansha Remote Control: A Best in Show winner.   Photo: Kathy Brown.

shown successfully throughout America and Canada.

THE RANCHLAKE KENNELS
Dorothy Warren of the famous Ranchlake kennels visited England and Crufts in 1992. She was known in England at the time because of her success in Akitas. Her first female was Am. Mexican, NSCA Ch. Ranchlake's Tamarisk Samsara, whose pet name was Seiko. From Seiko's first litter, of six puppies, five became American Champions. Seiko also obtained her Register of Merit. Dorothy's first stud dog was Ch. Prescott J's Chances Are, who proved to be a very worthy producer, passing on his vibrant red colour, his shortened body length and his added depth of chest to his progeny.

Dorothy's newest star is World Int. Puerto Rico, Am. Ch. Ranchlake's Rocket Man who, at 18 months of age, is Number Two Shiba in breed points in the US. He received his World Championship title from Japanese judge

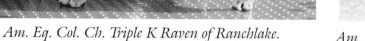
Am. Eq. Col. Ch. Triple K Raven of Ranchlake.

*Am. Mex. SKC, SCA, NSCA
Ch. Ranchlake Tamarisk
Samsara ROM.*

Hiroshi Kamisato. In the four years since Shibas were recognised by the AKC Dorothy has finished 15 Shibas and has four more pointed. Dorothy says that in her thirty years of experience showing dogs, the Japanese Shiba Inu has provided the greatest satisfaction as well as the most embarrassing moments.

NIPPO/USA POINT SYSTEM
This is used at the Shiba Classic Show, which is held annually by the Colonial Shiba Club Inc. and it is where Japanese judges officiate. It is printed in their catalogue.

SAIKOSHO: This is the highest award given. An automatic 15 point Championship is awarded to the Best Shiba In Show.

JUN SAIKOSHO: This is the second highest award and is given to the Best of Opposite Sex Shiba. This dog also receives an automatic 15 point Championship.

*World Int. Am.
Ch. Ranchlake's
Rocket Man*

Photo: Cook.

Each Class winner will be awarded
points as follows:

1st place	5 points
2nd place	4 points
3rd place	3 points
4th place	2 points

The points will be cumulative for
following years. Upon the accumulation
of 15 points, the dog will be titled
"Meiyosho" (Honorable).

14 THE INTERNATIONAL SHIBA INU

IRELAND

Soon after the arrival of the Japanese Shiba Inu in England, fanciers in Ireland took a very keen interest in the breed, frequently travelling over to shows and seminars, and carefully selecting foundation stock that would set up their own Shiba lines.

In Ireland the Irish Kennel Club is the governing body and it adheres to FCI rules. This means that Shibas bred in England and imported into Ireland have to be registered at the English Kennel Club and then registered at the Irish Kennel Club. They then can also compete at shows in Ireland, where Green Stars, the equivalent of Challenge Certificates, are on offer. Dogs born in Eire must be registered at the IKC and, if taken into England, re-registered at the Kennel Club in England. All dogs entered at Irish shows must be registered with the Irish Kennel Club before the date of the show.

The first Irish Shiba Champion was Madason Quicksilver at Nedraw, owned and shown by Fred Warden, who owns the Nedraw kennels. Fred Warden has

Madason Aka Moji Heru at Nedraw.

had dogs all his life, most notably breeding Rottweilers for more than thirty years, and producing numerous Champions in the breed. One of his most famous Rottweilers was owned by Joanne Yates, and was called Nedraw Black Sunshine. Fred judges the breed both in Ireland and in England. In 1988 he acquired his first pair of Shibas with whom he has had a great deal of success.

161

Madason Quicksilver at Nedraw: The first male Irish Champion.

Beckett Photography.

Fred also breeds Polish Lowlands with great success.

In 1992 Barbara Strickland gained the Champion's title with Madason Tarquin of Rossacre, and Fred Warden made up Madason Aka Moji Heru at Nedraw. The first bitch to win her crown in Ireland was Chris Barry's Azgard Koko San who, like the other dogs mentioned above, was also bred in England, at the Azgard Kennels.

Irish Champion Madason Aka Moji Heru of Nedraw was the first Shiba to appear in The Pedigree Chum Champion Stakes at Windsor and also to win the Any Variety Non-Separately Classified Stakes classes under Terry Thorn, to be followed the next year by Lizzie Dunhill's Vormund I'm Smartie winning AVNSC and going on to win Best In

Show at Richmond, also under Terry Thorn.

It was 1990 that the Irish Kennel Club allocated Green Stars to the breed. Shibas in Ireland are in the Pastoral Group. To achieve Championship status a dog has to receive 40 points. 20 of these points must consist of four 'majors' or five-point Green Stars under four different judges. After that the remaining points needed can be added to the 'majors' in ones and twos to make up the total of 40.

The value of Green Stars depends on the number of exhibits present on the day of the show. At Championship shows where two Green Stars are on offer, five dogs and five bitches must be present to allow the judge to award a 'major'. Where one Green Star is on offer to mixed classes, six dogs or bitches must be present to qualify for the five-point 'major'. When only one dog is present it can still be awarded one point towards the necessary 40. The St. Patrick's Day Show in March, held in Dublin, is the only show where a five-point Green Star is guaranteed, regardless of the number of dogs entered.

A judge in Ireland must be IKC approved. Fulfilling ring steward duties at shows helps towards being accepted as a judge. Would-be judges have to complete a questionnaire that is sent out by the IKC. Judges who have awarded Challenge Certificates or CACIBs abroad are usually accepted as judges in Ireland.

CONTINENTAL EUROPE

Many of the countries in Europe have fallen for the Shiba, importing them from various countries including Japan, America and England. With the less restricted movement which the Continent enjoys, dogs are able to travel from country to country for both showing and breeding purposes. Shibas are able to become Champions, and also International Champions, under the FCI rules. At the World Show held in Valencia, in Spain, in 1994 there were many Shibas competing. While the majority of Spain's Shibas are in the north, Ron Sterck, a well-known and well-respected Bull Terrier breeder, lives

The coming together of three countries: Int. Danish Ch. Kiskas Cinnamon at Madason (from England), her daughter, Int. Danish Ch. Kaissa's Hanna of Bonsai, and Kaissa's Chiisai Sanjyo (from Denmark), and Justa Wizard of Odds (from the USA). Photo: Kirsten Jorgensen.

*Int. Ch. Kiskas
Cinnamon at
Madason now living
in Denmark.*

*Photo: Kirsten
Jorgensen.*

in the South and he imported a male Shiba in 1992.

Some of the first Shiba Inus in Europe were introduced in 1972 by Mr and Mrs Carlsson of the famous Manloten Kennels in Sweden. They have, over the years, imported many Shibas from Japan. They have achieved a great success rate, notably with their home-bred Manlotens Tomodati who went Best In Show at a large Kennel Club event. In 1987 their Japanese import Benikatsura of Dairy Farm gained the title of Champion of Champions at an all breed Show in Sweden, making him the top winning Shiba in Sweden.

Another Manloten Champion is Manlotens Hashibami who resides in France and is owned and exhibited by Mr Leo Vasseur. In the table of top-

winning rare breeds, published recently, two English imports appeared for Shibas. They were Vormunds Annie's Song and Vormunds Jokers Wild. Lizzie Dunhill's Vormund Kennel is making quite an impact on the Continent in Shibas. Although this kennel is based in England, several of Lizzie Dunhill's dogs have been exported to the Continent, mainly to France, Belgium and Holland, where they have accumulated titles such as Top Rare Breed in France, Bundes Sieger and Siegerin, and several International Champion titles. Wellshim Black is Vormund is one of the most notable of the winners. He is shown, and proudly owned, by Dennis le Palen in France.

Shibas from the famous Romador-Perky Chow kennels owned by Maureen and Robert Dore in England were the foundation stock for Everett Verschoor in Holland. In the Netherlands, Cornelius Koot began breeding Shibas with stock brought from the Manloten and del Wasabi Kennels and had much success. Belgium's Bernard Dunglas of de Vaudival kennels has a lot of success in the breed.

Great strides have been made by Kirsten Jorgensen of the famous Kennel Kaissa in Denmark. Kirsten, well-known for her lovely Samoyeds, imported from England in 1990 Kiskas Cinnamon at Madason who was in-whelp to Madason Bonsai. A litter of seven puppies resulted. Cinnamon went on to gain her Danish and International title, as did a daughter from the resulting litter, and two males from it became DK Champions. Kaissa puppies are now spread across Europe, following in mother's footsteps. Kirsten also purchased Shibas from America and Sweden to take on her lines. On a recent visit to America, she visited Terry Arndt in Arizona and saw the famous Beni

Washi-Go, who was Cinnamon's father. Her most recent Shiba imports were purchased from Betty Scott in Prescott, Arizona.

A male, Madason Fanfare, who was one of the first Shibas in England to go Best in Show All Breeds – that was in 1991 – was sent to Hanna Laine Jensen, a top International judge. He became a Danish Champion and went on to sire several beautiful puppies both in Denmark and also in Southern Europe. One of them is Polish and Int. Ch. Kaissa's Chiisai Ringo, owned by Jadwiga Szulch. He also sired a grandchild of Cinnamon, DK Ch. Tronkaer's Amina Lotus, owned by Alice Christensen.

In Norway Christen Lang has had success with his Shibas from foundation stock sent from England by Roy Mulligan and H. Kadowaki of the Makota kennels. In Italy G. Chierra and D. Rorich of the del Wasabi Kennels have been breeding successfully for many years. Even as far afield as Israel the Shiba Inu has made an impact. Myrna

Int. Danish Ch.
Madason Fanfare.

Photo: Laine Jansen.

Shiboleth, famous for her Canaan Dogs, was smitten with the Shiba during a visit to England, and very soon after a Shiba puppy, from Fred Warden of the Nedraw kennels, was flying out on a plane to join her new owner, thus adding to the ever-growing band of Shiba lovers.

FCI SHOW REGULATIONS

With the ability to travel easily from country to country in Europe, a dog is able to also gain his International Title, having first gained his title in his own country. The show scene is very different to that in the UK. In the show ring you usually have the judge accompanied by a trainee judge; this is where would-be judges learn the art of judging. The trainee is there to observe procedure. Quite often the judge will explain, as he goes along, the finer points to the aspiring judge. *All* dogs are judged, and placed, and a critique done on every dog. They are graded Excellent, Very Good, Good and Bad.

The classification at shows is: Puppy Class; Junior Class; Young Dogs Class; Open Class; Working Class; Champions Class; Senior Class; Progeny Class; Breeding Class and Junior Handling. Dogs from Puppy classes do not compete for CAC or CACIBs. Junior, Young, Senior Dogs aged 7-10 years and Veterans over 10 years do not compete for the CACIBs. The CAC are awarded to the Best Male and the Best Bitch in the Winners class, and the CACIB may be given to the best male and the best bitch entered in the Open class, Working class or the Champions class.

AUSTRALIA

The Australians have also taken the Shiba to their hearts. Arthur Lane is one of the most notable influences on the breed there. He has been in the dog world for 45 years, and 20 of those years he has spent judging dogs throughout Japan and South East Asia. He is internationally well-known. Arthur first saw the Shiba in 1974 and was determined that he would, at some time, own and exhibit one and popularise the breed in Australia. In 1990 that dream became a reality and his kennels in Melbourne flourished. Arthur Lane has served on the Committee of the Kennel Control Council in Victoria for over 20 years. Mostly the dogs imported into Australia came from Japan but some came from England. As the breed's popularity grew, so did the band of enthusiasts. Many Japanese judges have visited and judged at shows, passing on their expertise and knowledge.

T*HE FINAL WORD*

The Shiba has been part of the Japanese culture for centuries. The Japanese have nurtured and loved the breed. Their devotion to their Japanese Native Dog and his characteristics is plain for all to see. These dogs are greatly prized and guarded. We owe it to the Japanese people to maintain and perpetuate their vision of what a Shiba should be. It is all too easy to wander from the path of what is correct and of what constitutes perfection. We have good foundations to work on and must go forward, adhering to what is laid down in the Standard for the Breed. The Japanese have a saying about special relationships. They say 'our hearts touched'. When you have a Shiba your hearts will touch *forever*.

GLOSSARY

ALMOND EYES: Oval-shaped like an almond, slanted at the corners.

ANGULATION: Angles that are formed by lines and joints. Front and rear assemblies are particularly important, as are shoulders, stifles and hock joints.

BARREL-CHESTED: Rounded chest shape.

BENCHED: A show at which the dogs have to be leashed to a bench while out of the ring.

BITE: Meeting of the teeth, when the jaw is closed.

BLAZE: White markings running down the forehead to muzzle.

BODIED UP: Well-developed.

BREAST BONE: Bone running down the middle of the chest to which all but the floating ribs are attached.

BRISKET: Area of chest between the forelegs including the breastbone.

BROOD BITCH: A bitch that is kept for breeding.

BRUSH: A bushy tail.

BUTTON EARS: Semi-erected ears, folding over at their tips.

CANINES: The two upper and the two lower fang-like teeth (behind the incisors).

CARPALS: Pastern joint bones.

CASTRATED: When a male's testicles are removed.

CHEST: The body enclosed by the ribs.

COBBY: Short-bodied and compact.

CONDITION: Health of the dog, shown by coat, weight, appearance and deportment.

CONFORMATION: Form and structure, make-up and shape of the dog. The arrangement of the parts in conformance with the Breed Standard.

COW-HOCKED: When hock joints turn towards each other, causing the feet to turn out.

CROUP: Part of back above the hindlegs and pelvis, in front of tail-set.

CRYPTORCHID: An adult dog whose testicles have not descended into the scrotum.

DAM: The mother of a litter of puppies.

DEWCLAWS: A claw on the inside of the legs, often removed in young puppies in some breeds, but not in Shibas.

DISQUALIFY: A decision made by a judge or show committee, ruling that a dog has a condition making it ineligible

for competition under dog show rules
under the breed's Standard.

DISTEMPER TEETH: Teeth marked,
pitted, ringed and often stained due to a
distemper or other severe infection.

DOUBLE COAT: Guard hairs
protruding through softer insulating
layer beneath.

DRIVE: A solid thrusting of the hindquarters denoting sound locomotion.

ELBOW: The upper arm and forearm
joint.

ENTROPION: A condition in which
the eyelids turn inwards causing the eyelashes to irritate the eye-ball.

EVEN BITE: Meeting of the upper and
the lower front teeth with no overlap.

EXPRESSION: The general appearance
of the front of the head, as typical of the
breed.

EYE-TEETH: The upper canines.

FEATHERING: Longer hair fringing
on ears and tail.

FLANK: The body area between the last
rib and the hip.

FLAT WITHERS: A fault that is the
result of short upright shoulder blades
that abruptly join the withers.

FOREARM: The foreleg bone between
the elbow and the pastern.

FOREFACE: The front part of the head
in front of the eyes and the muzzle.

FURROW: Median line down centre of
skull to the stop.

GAIT: A style of movement – running or
trotting.

GESTATION: The period when the
pups are developing inside the mother.

GROOM: To brush, comb and prepare a
dog for exhibition or done for pleasure.

GUARD HAIRS: Coarser outer hairs.
HACKLES: Hair on the neck or back that rises when the dog is showing aggression or fear.
HANDLER: A person that handles, shows or exhibits a dog at shows or in trials.
HARE-FOOT: Relatively long and narrow feet.
HAUNCHES: The back part of the thigh on which the dog sits.
HAW : A third eyelid or membrane in the inside corner of the eye.
HEAT: Seasonal period of the female; normally this occurs every six months.
HEIGHT: Dog's height measured from the ground to the top of the shoulder.
HINDQUARTERS: The rear anatomy of the dog – pelvis, thighs, hocks and paws.
HIP DYSPLASIA: Malformation of the ball and socket joint in the dog's hips.

HOCKS: Joints in the hind limbs below the knees or stifle joints, the dog's heel.
IN-BREEDING: Mating within the same family – e.g. a bitch mated to her sons or a dog to his daughters.
INCISORS: The upper and lower teeth between the canines at the front of the dog's mouth.
IN SEASON: On heat ready for mating.
JOWLS: The fleshy part of the lips and jaws.
LEVEL BITE: When the front teeth incisors of the upper and lower jaws meet edge to edge.
LINE BREEDING: The mating of related dogs of the same line or family, to a common ancestor – e.g. a dog to his grand-dam.
LOINS: The part of the body between the last rib and the back legs.
MANE: Long hair around the neck.

MASK: Dark, mask-like shading on the head.

MATE: The breeding of dog and bitch.

MILK TEETH: First teeth. Puppies lose these at four to six months of age.

MOLARS: Dogs have two molars on each side of the upper jaw and three on each side of the lower jaw.

MUZZLE: The part of the head containing the mouth and nose, the portion of the head in front of the eyes.

OCCIPUT: Upper, back part of the skull.

OVARY: Two reproduction glands in the female.

OVER-REACHING: Fault in the trot caused by more angulation and drive from behind than in front, so that the rear feet are forced to step to one side of the forefeet to avoid touching.

OVER-SHOT: When the upper teeth project beyond the lower.

PADS: The tough, cushioned soles of the feet.

PASTERN: Lower part of the leg between the wrist (carpus) and the digits (foot).

PATELLA: A cap-like bone at the stifle joint (similar to the knee-cap).

PUPPY: A dog under twelve months of age.

REACH OF FRONT: Length of forward stride taken by forelegs without wasted or excessive motion.

REGISTER: To record details of dog's breeding with the respective Kennel Club.

ROACHED: A convex arching of the back.

RUFF: Long thick hair encircling the neck.

SADDLE: Black hairs marking the shape of a saddle on the dog's back.

SCAPULA: The shoulder blade.

SCISSOR BITE: A bite in which the upper front teeth slightly overlap the lower front teeth.

SHORT-COUPLED: Short between the rib and hip joint forming short loins.

SIRE: The father of a litter of puppies.

SKULL: Bony framework of the head.

SMOOTH-COATED: Short sleek hair lying close to the skin.

SOUNDNESS: The state of mental and physical health when all organs and faculties are functioning normally.

SPAYING: When a female's ovaries and uterus are removed.

SPLAYED FEET: Toes that are spread wide apart.

SPRING OF RIB: Curvature of ribs for heart and lung capacity.

STANCE: Manner of standing.

STAND-OFF COAT: Long heavy coat standing out from the body.

STANDARD: The standard of perfection for each breed.

STIFLE: Joint of hindleg, between the thigh and second thigh, the angle of which is important in Breed Standards.

STOP: Depression between and in front of the eyes, where the skull and nasal bone meet.

STRAIGHT HOCKS: Hocks that are vertical.

STUD: Males that are used for breeding.

STUD BOOK: A record of the breeding particulars of recognised breeds.

TESTICLES: Two genital glands of the male.

THIGH: Hindquarters from hip joint to stifle.

TICKING: Coat pattern in which spots of colours stand out against the basic background colour.

TOPLINE: The outline of the dog from behind the withers to the tail-set.

TROT: A two-beat diagonal gait in which the feet at diagonally opposite ends of the body strike the ground together, right hind with left front and left hind with right front.

TRIM: Grooming that entails clipping or plucking.

TYPEY: Characteristic qualities distinguishing the breed. Essential embodiment of the standard.

UNDERSHOT: Having the lower jaw projecting. The opposite of overshot.

UPPER ARM: The humerus or foreleg bone between the shoulder blade and the forearm.

VENT: Both the anal opening and the small area of light hair directly beneath the tail.

WHELPING: Giving birth to puppies.

WHELPS: New-born puppies.

WITHERS: The highest point of the shoulders, just behind the neck.

WRY MOUTH: Mouth in which the lower jaw is not in line with the upper.

SOME ABBREVIATIONS EXPLAINED

AI Artificial Insemination
AKC American Kennel Club
ANKC Australian National Kennel Club
AOC Any other colour
AVNSC Any Variety Not Separately Classified
B Bitch
BIS Best in Show
BOS Best Opposite Sex
BOB Best of Breed
CAC Certificat d'aptitude au Championnat de Beauté
CACIB Certificat d'aptitude au

Championnat International de Beauté
CC Challenge Certificate
CD Companion Dog
Ch. Champion
CKC Canadian Kennel Club
D Dog
FCI Fédération Cynologique
Internationale
Int. Ch. International Champion
JKC The Japanese Kennel Club
KC The UK Kennel Club
NAF Name applied for
NIPPO The Nihon Ken Hozonkai (The
Japanese Dog Preservation Society)
UK Utility Dog
UDEX Utility Dog Excellent

USEFUL ADDRESSES
The Kennel Club
105 Clarges Street
Piccadilly
London W1Y 8AB
Tel: 0171 629 5828

The American Kennel Club
51, Madison Avenue
New York NY 10010, USA
Tel: 212 696 8200
and
5580 Centreview Dr Ste 200,
Raleigh,USA
NC 27606-3390

Australian National Kennel Council
The Royal Showgrounds
Ascot Vale, 3032 Victoria, Australia
Tel: 0061 11 76 33

Dansk Kennelklub
Parkvej 1, Jersie Strand
DK-2680 Solrod Strand, Denmark
Tel: 0045 53 14 15 66

Japan Kennel Club
N1-5, Kanda, Suda-cho,
Chiyoda-Ku
Tokyo 101, Japan

Irish Kennel Club
Fottrell House, Unit 36
Greenmount Office Park
Dublin 6W, Eire
Tel: 00 353 533 300

Fédération Cynologique Internationale
Rue Leopold 11, 14 B-6530
Thuin
Belgium
Tel: 071 59 12 28

Belgian Kennel Club
Société Royale Saint-Hubert
Avenue de l'Armée 25
B-11040
Brussels
Tel: 03202 732 40 05

Norsk Kennelklub
Nils Hansens Vei 20
Box 163 Bryn, N-0611
Oslo 6
Tel: 0047 2 65 60 00

The Nihon Ken Hozonkai
Kenkyusha Building 2F
2-9 Kanda Surugadai,
Chiyoda-ku
Tokyo 101
Japan

For names and addresses of the individual Shiba Clubs in each of the above countries contact the Kennel Clubs listed. They will put you in touch with the Clubs' Secretaries. Most Shiba Clubs issue a newsletter or journal. Membership of the Club will get you on the mailing list. Schedules of Club Shows and events are also available from the individual Breed Clubs, as is information about the welfare and rescue services.